244735

D0007261

CHILD IDENTITY THEFT

CHILD IDENTITY THEFT

WHAT EVERY PARENT NEEDS TO KNOW

Robert P. Chappell, Jr.

ROWMAN & LITTLEFIELD PUBLISHERS, INC.
Lanham • Boulder • New York • Toronto • Plymouth, UK

Published by Rowman & Littlefield Publishers, Inc.
A wholly owned subsidary of The Rowman & Littlefield Publishing Group, Inc.
4501 Forbes Boulevard, Suite 200, Lanham, Maryland 20706
www.rowman.com

10 Thornbury Road, Plymouth PL6 7PP, United Kingdom

British Library Cataloguing in Publication Information Available

Library of Congress Cataloging-in-Publication Data

Chappell, Robert P.
   Child identity theft : what every parent needs to know / Robert P. Chappell, Jr.
      p. cm.
   Includes bibliographical references and index.
   ISBN 978-1-4422-1862-8 (cloth : alk. paper) — ISBN 978-1-4422-1864-2 (electronic)
   1. Identity theft—United States . 2. Identity theft—United States—Prevention.
I. Title.
   HV6679.C428 2013
   332.024—dc23

                                                            2012036123

Printed in the United States of America

CONTENTS

FOREWORD

King F. Davis, Jr.

When Bob Chappell asked me to write the foreword for his book, I was visiting my daughter, son-in-law, and grandson at their home in the heart of the Blue Ridge Mountains in beautiful Roanoke, Virginia. This is also where Bob Chappell serves as the field lieutenant for a division headquarters of the Virginia State Police. I have known Bob for fifteen years, both as an Army officer and as a fellow law enforcement officer. Although I had not seen him for several years, we have always stayed in touch. I was happy, no, eager, to accept his request.

Bob Chappell is one of the most talented, hardworking, sincere, and patriotic servants to the citizens of this country and the Commonwealth of Virginia. When I first met Bob, I was a Colonel, Special Forces, U.S. Army Reserve, and had just taken command of the 2d Brigade of the Army Reserve's 80th Division (Blue Ridge Division). The division headquarters is located in Richmond, Virginia, and the 2d Brigade's headquarters is in Roanoke/Salem, Virginia.

Bob was a young Army Reserve Captain and the Aide de Camp for the division commander. He had a tough job. The Commanding General (CG) was a demanding "old-school"-type soldier who ran the division with an iron hand. He clearly wanted the entire division to live up to the Army's old recruiting slogan, "Be all you can be." He drove himself hard and expected the same from those that worked for him.

At the time, my civilian job was as an assistant to the special agent in charge of the U.S. Secret Service's Washington, D.C., field office. Further, I was on loan to the Baltimore/Washington High Intensity Drug Trafficking Area as agent in charge of a multijurisdictional counterdrug task force. As you might guess, my civilian job was intense, time consuming, and dangerous. That, coupled with handling Army issues at lunch, odd times of my day, evenings, and weekends, left me nearly worn out and somewhat frazzled. I wasn't the only one in that boat. The other brigade commanders and division staff officers were equally, or even more, successful and busy at their civilian jobs and equally, or even more, pressured with Army business.

Since Bob went with the general almost everywhere and seemed to be doing Army duties continuously, I assumed that he had to be either a full-time, active-duty National Guard/reservist, had a part-time job, or at least had a job that allowed him almost unlimited time to tend to his Army duties. He made the Energizer Bunny look like a couch potato. A few weeks later I was astounded when he told me that we had law enforcement careers in common and that he was a Virginia state trooper, also assigned to a counterdrug squad.

Within law enforcement circles, the Virginia State Police is known as an outstanding organization. Its troopers are elite, thoroughly screened, well trained, and highly professional. The Virginia State Police does not take a backseat to any other law enforcement agency, federal, state, or local. I had been impressed with Bob Chappell before, but after finding out about his civilian position, I was in awe of this young officer.

As time went on, my assessment and praise for Bob increased severalfold. When his tour as Aide de Camp was finished, I sought him out to be the S-1 (head of the administrative staff) for the 2d Brigade. This was in spite of the fact that he was a Captain and the position called for a Major. With Bob as the S-1, the 2d Brigade led the division, and even the Army Reserve, in on-time and complete officer and noncommissioned officer evaluation reports, recruiting, and military occupational specialty (MOS) qualification. These were problem areas that seemed unsolvable throughout the Army Reserve. Yet, Bob's talent; passion; skill in working with people; and amazing, indefatigable drive enabled him to find and institute solutions that were the envy of other units.

In 1999, after I retired from the Army Reserve, I kept in contact with Bob. As an Army officer, he was promoted to Major, then Lieutenant Colonel, and took command of a battalion in the 2d Brigade. His battalion was eventually deployed to Iraq, where he led soldiers with distinction.

After retirement, I became a police chief in Los Angeles County and tried to steal Bob away to fill a vacant sergeant's position. His loyalty to the Virginia State Police kept him in his home state and led to his promotion to sergeant, first sergeant, and then lieutenant, with extensive experience in both patrol and investigative assignments.

When Bob first told me that he was writing a book, I told him that I had started to write one about my experiences in the Secret Service but got stuck and never seemed to be able to finish. My question was, "How did you do it? What motivated you to press through to the last period?"

His answer . . . "The information that I was writing about is so important to the youth of this nation and their parents that I HAD to complete the book!"

That was a powerful statement, and I had to know more. As a Secret Service agent and police chief, I have been associated with the investigation of several cases of identity theft. Those cases involved the identities of persons with the same or similar names, or deceased persons, but I was not aware of the magnitude or severe ramifications of child identity theft. Over the next hour, Bob kept my family and me enthralled with vital information that we needed to know. My daughter and son-in-law were especially interested, since they have a two-year-old son and will likely have more children in the future. As a grandparent, I was astonished by what I learned and am convinced that you will be too.

Among other things, Bob explained how child identities have become vulnerable due to the way Social Security numbers are issued and how births, and deaths, are recorded and announced. He explained the ease with which credit, credit cards, and bank accounts are granted to the spotless backgrounds of children. He also explained how these criminals avoid detection because, unlike adults, children never check their credit scores or review bank statements, credit card accounts, or other financial statements. Bob also pointed out how these cases can cover the activities of gangs and terrorists groups. In other words, child identity theft is relevant to all of us. Plus, the impact of these crimes is far reaching and potentially devastating.

I'm sure you will enjoy and benefit from reading this book written by a truly good person with a passion for the safety and well-being of his fellow man.

King F. Davis, Jr.
Glendora, California
September 2012

ACKNOWLEDGMENTS

To those who have loved and supported me during the writing of this book, and in life, I say thank you.

To Julie Christine, whose love and support is my driving force in life.

To Leslie Danielle, who provides sunshine in my heart each and every day.

To Elizabeth Michelle, who was the first to bring me the joy of being a father.

To Megan and Jesse, who keep me young at heart.

To my mother, Florine Chappell, who has provided me with unconditional love her entire life.

To the memory of my late father, Robert P. Chappell, Sr., whom I love and miss deeply.

To my sister, Tamara, who shares my kindred spirit. I love you very much.

To my sister, Cindy, who diligently cares for our mother, I love you and thank you.

To my nephew and niece, Willem and Claire, for their love of "Uncle Bob."

To my aunts, Sheila, Mary, Marjorine, Bessie, Janette, and Beatrice, who have loved me over the years.

To my late Uncle James Chappell, a great man who loved America. My service with the 101st Airborne in Iraq was in memory of you.

To my late Uncle Russell Chappell who loved me, treating me as one of his own children.

To my lifelong friend Ron "Keith" Farley.

To my good friend and supporter, Marilyn McCurdy.

To my agent, Claire Gerus, who believed in me and gave me the strength to realize my dream of publishing this book.

To Rowman & Littlefield Publishing Group for your part in helping to make my dream a success.

To King F. Davis, Jr., for his willingness to write the foreword and his kind words.

To one of the greatest leaders and mentors I have ever had the privilege to work for in all my years in law enforcement, Captain Steven L. Chumley of the Virginia State Police. God blessed me with the opportunity to learn from you.

To the members of the Virginia State Police who faithfully serve the Commonwealth of Virginia.

To the members of the Virginia State Police Color Guard team, both past and present, for your dedication to our mission.

To those who helped make me successful in the Virginia State Police Division 1 during my tenure there:

- Commonwealth of Virginia—Secretary of Public Safety Marla Graff Decker
- Virginia State Police—Lt. Tom Bradshaw, Sgt. Alan Chambers, Sgt. Chris Clark, Colonel W. Steven Flaherty, Lt. J.C. Lewis, F/Sgt. Ray Newby, F/Sgt. Hans Rehme, Lt. John Ruffin, Sgt. Kevin Satterfield, F/Sgt. Michele Ticho, and Sgt. Marilyne Wilson
- Virginia Capitol Police—Lieutenant John McKee
- Henrico County Police (Virginia)—Captain Chris Alberta

ACKNOWLEDGMENTS

- Richmond City Police (Virginia)—Lieutenant Colonel John Buturla, Major Steve Drew

To my good friend Lieutenant Curtis Hardison, who has always had my back in life.

To Trooper Landon Umberger, who keeps my legacy alive.

To the many secretaries who have supported me in my career and made me successful behind the scenes.

To my career-long friends in law enforcement, Chief Don Goodman (Radford, Virginia), VSP First Sergeant Frank Pyanoe, Captain Tim Guthrie (Salem, Virginia), Special Agent Glenn Thompson (CSX Railroad Police Department), Special Agent Steve Butcher (U.S. Secret Service), and Officer Shelly Benac (U.S. Capitol Police).

To Chief Kim Crannis and the officers of the Blacksburg Virginia Police Department, where I started my career in law enforcement.

To Chief Wendell Flinchum, Major Kevin Foust, Major Gene Deisinger, Captain Joey Albert, Captain Vince Houston, and the officers of the Virginia Tech Police Department. Go Hokies!

To my fellow graduates of the National Criminal Justice Command College, University of Virginia, for your commitment to enhancing public safety through leadership. A special thanks to Cynthia Orshek for your encouragement and support.

To the members who served on the Rockbridge Regional Drug Task Force with me and made my role as Drug Task Force Coordinator a success: Hugh Bolen, Stan Bush, Gary Coleman, Tony McFaddin, Jay Patterson, Doug Pugh, Mark Riley, and Rob Tackett.

To our brave service men and women serving around the world protecting our freedom, and to the United Service Organization (U.S.O.), which has always been there for both the service personnel and their families.

To those who believed in, mentored, and guided me in my military career: Major General (Retired) Max Guggenheimer, Colonel (Retired) King F.

Davis, Colonel (Retired) Kurt J. Jenne, and CW4 (Retired) Phil Culbertson.

To my Army Reserve buddy, Lieutenant Colonel Wesley Huff, who served with me both stateside and in Iraq. Hooah!

To Sandra and Dudley Howard (Rixeyville, Virginia) for their patriotic support during my service in Iraq.

To Colonel (Retired) Frank Blakely and the staff of the United States Army War College in Carlisle, Pennsylvania, for providing me with an outstanding education in pursuit of my Master of Strategic Studies degree.

To the 47th Combat Support Hospital, stationed in Mosul, Iraq, during my tour overseas, for the outstanding medical care provided to me.

To Christopher L. Lentz, PA, Veteran's Medical Center, Salem, Virginia, for providing me with the best medical care a soldier could ever ask for. You are an honor to your profession.

Lastly, to Sergeant First Class Kevin Bellow of the Texas National Guard, who cared for me immediately after I was injured in Iraq, even though he was injured himself; the true test of an outstanding American soldier.

To anyone whom I may have inadvertently overlooked in my acknowledgments of appreciation, I apologize, as my heart was in the right place and I am grateful for your support.

1

UNDERSTANDING CHILD IDENTITY THEFT

Chapter 1 of this book provides you with an explanation of exactly what child identity theft is. It also gives alarming facts and statistics about child identity theft, America's fastest-growing crime committed against children.

QUESTION #1: WHAT EXACTLY IS CHILD IDENTITY THEFT?

Child identity theft is the use of a child's identity or personal information by someone other than the child for personal gain or enrichment. A child's identity or private information might consist of their name, address, date of birth, Social Security number, birth certificate details, death certificate information, or any other information descriptive of the child, which represents or represented them as a particular individual.

As we'll discuss in the next chapter, child identity theft is growing rapidly as more criminals see its benefits. The difference between stealing a child's identity and an adult's identity is the former's "shelf-life appeal," that is, the likelihood that the theft of personal information from a child will go undetected for a longer period of time. If you've attempted to obtain a home loan recently, you know that it is a slow and cumbersome process. A thief needs to steal an identity that the owner will not be checking every thirty days. With a child's Social Security number, a thief not only gets a clean credit history, but it's likely the crime won't be discovered until the child grows up and applies for credit or a student loan.

There are two types of child identity theft: financial and criminal. In financial identity theft, the perpetrator uses the child's Social Security number and/or name to open new lines of credit. Contrary to popular belief, credit issuers currently do not have a system in place to verify the age of the applicant. They also do not ask for other identification to determine whether the name and Social Security number are a match. This loophole has created an opportunity for scammers and thieves, and consumer groups are pushing to have it closed by creating a verification system, as I will discuss later in this book.

Criminal identity theft is committed when someone "borrows," or permanently steals, the identifying information of a child. The information obtained is then used to obtain a license, medical insurance, or employment, or it may even be used in the commission of a crime. This often happens in cases where someone had their license revoked and is seeking a new one, or when an illegal immigrant is trying to qualify for a job in the United States.

One of the reasons child identity theft has become so prevalent is because awareness of its existence is lacking. Many parents fail to realize the danger and do not know what questions to ask, which means the crime can remain undetected for years. Under normal circumstances, for example, you would never wonder if your child had a mortgage or a bankruptcy in another state. And if he or she did, would you know what to do?

Yet these are precisely the issues that arise when child identity theft occurs. Take Nathan, a typical victim, who later sought professional help in clearing his name. According to an article published by AllClear ID Alert Network,[1] when Nathan was fourteen years old, his parents discovered he was $600,000 in debt. In addition to showing numerous credit cards in collection, his credit report included a foreclosure on a home fraudulently purchased in his name years earlier by the person who stole his identity.

Home mortgages are but one of many purchases thieves target with your child's information. There are others, and I will discuss them in upcoming chapters. Good credit buys automobiles, high-dollar electronics, and furniture. It also buys vacations, jewelry, and more. The thieves can be strangers or someone you or your child knows.

Larry, for example, was nineteen years old when he discovered his identity had been stolen several years earlier. According to *Good Morning America*,[2] not only was he $100,000 in debt, but he had a $41,000 mortgage. Tragically, he later discovered that the identity thief was his father. Now twenty-eight years old, he's spent the last nine years trying to clean up his credit. He still hasn't turned his father in to the police.

Larry's case is not an isolated incident, as you will read later in the book when I cover the emotional trauma of child identity theft committed by relatives. Identity thieves come from all walks of life. Our economy has weakened, and the instances of relatives "borrowing" a child's identity have risen. That a relative would steal from a child is unbelievable, but it happens daily. Parents have the responsibility to care for children. Sometimes, though, stealing occurs as parents fall on hard times.

Each child needs to realize that a child's identity is his or her own. Their personal descriptive information is not meant to be shared or held in joint. Children share many characteristics and commonalities with their parents— things like physical appearance, a home address, telephone number, likes and dislikes, tastes, or beliefs. Children will also share commonalities with other children, such as birthdays, schools attended, sports participated in, church memberships, or friendships.

Regardless of what we have in common with someone else, however, our federal, state, and local laws require that each person be unique, identifiable, and separate. This is the driving force behind the development of a Social Security number that is unique to each person and never intentionally duplicated.

If you ask any victim, or parent of a victim, of child identity theft, they will say that it is a devastating crime and a life-changing event. When you have something as personal as your identity stolen from you, it shatters your sense of security, and it can take years to undo the damage. Your identity is your life. While it may be just a name to someone else, to you it is everything.

QUESTION #2: HOW BIG OF A PROBLEM IS CHILD IDENTITY THEFT?

While books on child identity theft are almost nonexistent, statistics on identity theft are plentiful. A recent report from Javelin Strategy and Research[3] identified 9.9 million Americans who became victims of ID theft. These thefts resulted in the loss of 48 billion dollars. According to *ABC News/ Money*, "depending upon the study or report you read, from 140,000 to more than 400,000 young people per year become victims of a crime that may not necessarily impact their daily lives when it occurs, but can have devastating long-term financial and emotional repercussions."[4]

The federal agency responsible for tracking identity theft and child identity theft is the Federal Trade Commission (FTC). FTC data shows that historically 5 percent of all American victims are children, and this number is increasingly rising. According to a Carnegie Mellon CyLab Child Identity Theft Study,[5] a survey of 40,000 children found that 4,000 of their identities had been compromised (10 percent).

Child identity theft is much more complex than identity theft involving adults. In the chapters of this book, we will help parents fully understand why children are targeted instead of adults, what constitutes child identity theft, and who is targeting and stealing children's identities. We will look at a new term called "*identity* cloning," as well as the targeting of children with passports, foster children, and children of certain demographics. This book will also help parents decide when is the best time, among the many options, to obtain a child's Social Security number.

We also look heavily at preventive measures that you can proactively take to protect your child and all school students. These measures include parents and teachers sitting down with their children and students to discuss what "private" information is; online security; obtaining your child's credit report; opting out on business transactions; registering in the National Do Not Call Registry; shredding documents; and being alert for scams.

The information in this book includes sections to assist you in the reporting process should your child become a victim. A step-by-step guide is crucial, as your family will be devastated, overwhelmed, and in need of guidance through the web of agencies that need to be notified. You will also need emotional support and counseling for both you and your child.

Yes, child identity theft really is that big of a problem. When the economy is bad, criminal behavior increases. Identity theft has become so prevalent that the Gallup Organization conducted a poll that revealed "One in six Americans say they have had financial information—such as their bank or credit card numbers—stolen."[6] Think about it for a moment: if you lose your wallet or purse, what is also lost? Lost are our child's photos, insurance card, and probably their Social Security card or number.

The statistics are of great concern, but they do not paint the entire picture. When times are hard, parents do things they will later regret, such as borrowing their child's identity. Most parental and family identity theft does not get reported; therefore, as bad as the statistics may be, they are not capturing all that is happening. Society is starting to understand identity theft, and efforts to educate the public are developing. Statistics show, however, that even with the push commercial companies and federal government agencies have made toward identity theft protection, child identity theft is on the rise, untouched by their efforts. This leads us to ask why thieves are targeting children.

QUESTION #3: WHY DO THIEVES TARGET CHILDREN?

KSL TV 5 of Salt Lake City published a story on April 11, 2011, titled "Protecting Kids against ID Theft a Grim Reality."[7] In this article, a representative of the Utah Attorney General's Office was quoted as saying, "We're seeing at least 75 percent of our reports child identity theft related." What they are trying to convey to both Utah and the rest of America is that identity theft against children is growing at an alarming rate, and 75 percent of all of their cases now involve children as victims. According to the Utah representative, "Child identity theft in Utah is significant and growing mainly because the state has a lot of kids." The truth is that every state has a lot of children, and all are at risk. Utah is just one of the many states awakening to the issue.

The Carnegie Mellon CyLab[8] research previously referenced also shows that in fact children have a fifty-one times greater attack rate than do adults. So why are thieves targeting children at such a high rate? The answer is simple when you understand how the system of issuing credit works. In the world of credit issuance the "cleaner" your credit history record, the greater chance you will be approved for credit cards, get loans approved, or get a positive recommendation or endorsement for revolving credit. You are essentially approved because the credit reporting agencies have nothing negative in your credit file.

The second factor has to do with discovering the fraud abuse. Most adults are technologically savvy, having hooked up with online banking and mobile phone, BlackBerry, or iPhone applications that allow them to check their bank accounts, directly access their credit card accounts, and view account statements. Even those adults without such technology look at their daily mail, read their monthly bank statements, and pay close attention to who calls their home phones.

Parents routinely pay monthly home utility bills, phone bills, cable bills, and Internet access bills. Parents pay personal revolving credit bills for items such as furniture and appliances bought with monthly installment accounts. Children do not do any of the above-mentioned activities. They live the lives of children, which involves playing, learning, and developing.

Children are financially innocent, which encompasses not paying monthly bills or worrying about jobs, income, and retirement. Unfortunately for child victims of identity theft, parents can be caught in this same dangerous, cyclic mindset. Parents have the ability to uncover the crime of child identity theft just by proactively obtaining a copy of their child's credit report. If a child has a credit report, that itself is a red flag.

Parents love their children and seek to protect them as they grow. For eighteen years, parents work daily to guide their children into the world of "adulthood." Along the way, though, parents believe their children should have no financial responsibilities, worries, or concerns. It is this mindset that keeps parents from deciphering that their child has been victimized.

Criminals like children because they are free of debt, clear of any bad record, unsuspecting as a target, and unlikely to generate concern as long as the criminal diverts mailings away from the child's real address. This crime is not usually discovered until the child becomes an adult and applies for their first credit card, fills out an employment application where a credit check is done, or applies for admission to a college.

As to the riddle of why thieves target children, I say that the answer is found in another question. Would you rather steal the identity of an adult who will most likely see the signs of theft in their monthly bills and bank statements or the identity of a child who will not see the theft for up to eighteen years?

QUESTION #4: ISN'T IDENTITY THEFT SOMETHING ONLY RICH PEOPLE HAVE TO WORRY ABOUT?

A common misconception has been that you have to be rich to be a target for identity thieves. A lot of people believe that only adults need to worry about identity theft. This is far from the truth, as fame, fortune, and age have very little to do with why child identity theft victims become the prime choice. It has to do more with the accessibility of information, the likelihood of being discovered in the criminal act, and the attractiveness of a target having a new, unused, or a good credit history.

On May 11, 2011, I turned the television on to see a tearful teenager talking about how child identity theft criminals should go to jail. The show was NBC's *Today* and they covered how this juvenile, and three others just like her, were thousands of dollars in debt with mortgages, auto loans, credit cards, utility bills, and even bankruptcies. All of these children were victims of child identity theft.

The tearful girl, now a teen, owed $750,000 for homes and automobiles that thieves had purchased using her personal information. Most people watching the TV show most likely asked themselves how this could have happened. I knew what happened, as I was aggressively researching and studying crime trends, as well as compiling information in recent years on child identity theft. This crime, and my findings, will both astonish and horrify parents. I hope to provide preventive education to my readers to reduce the number of instances of child identity theft.

As I watched this teenager cry, the reporter revealed that her theft had actually occurred back when she was only three years old. What was worse was that her information had been stolen, sold, resold, and then sold again. The teen couldn't understand how something illegal could go unsolved.

The cameras left the teen to zoom in on two male subjects working at jobs. The first thief was an auto-body repairman working just miles from the victim's house. He was confronted in the parking lot of the auto-body shop, and he stated he did not want to talk about it. Supposedly, he would have his attorney contact the reporter; it never happened. As the TV interview continued, the teen was then joined by her father. Her father was visibly frustrated at how such an act of child identity theft could have happened, yet go unpunished.

Unpunished it is, as the report continues to cover a story on a second suspect who used the identity of the same teenage victim at a "99-cents" store. The reporters encounter this thief as he gathers shopping carts outside the business. He claims not to know how credit reports show that he took out several auto loans using the teen victim's Social Security number. In a move clearly to avoid the discussion, he only replied with "I don't know" when he was asked to comment on why he victimized the child.

Consider this: Why was the teen in the NBC story targeted? At the time of the theft, the victim was only three years old. She had no job, no money, and no wealth. From the perspective of law enforcement, she was targeted because she had something more valuable than parents understand: a good credit history.

Criminals want a target that does not have a credit history filled with late bill payments, bankruptcy, foreclosure, or abuse. Thieves want their fraudulent application to be the first one received by the credit agency under the name and information submitted, thus ensuring issuance of credit and a clear path to maximum purchases. This good credit history translated for this victim into a successful scam where thieves were able to obtain credit cards, auto loans, and a home mortgage, all using her personal information.

QUESTION #5: WHO STEALS A CHILD'S IDENTITY?

A wide range of thieves steal children's identities. Individuals who target children for this crime include opportunists, scammers, terrorists, organized crime ring members, and profit-motivated criminals. Unfortunately, thieves who use children's identities also include parents, relatives, and caregivers. The FTC states in their Identity Theft Survey Report[9] that 16 percent of all victims know their thief. The breakdown of persons who commit this crime, according to the survey, is as follows: 6 percent family members, 2 percent coworkers, 8 percent friends, neighbors, or in-home employees, and 84 percent people unknown to the victim.

Thieves who are strangers to the child just need to figure out the best way to access the information. The first question thieves usually ask themselves is, can I get the information without meeting the child face-to-face? While a face-to-face conversation with a child can yield the information thieves desire, such as name, date of birth, and address, it exposes the thief to potential discovery.

The average parent reading this book about child identity theft for the first time might feel that obtaining a child's identity information is difficult, as they are not "connected" to the world of finance or public records. This is far from the truth. As mentioned above, thieves who are strangers to the child will seek first to steal the information without contact, such as by stealing school records, medical office records, dental or orthodontist office records, recreational sports records, worship or church office records, or through home invasions while the family is away.

If contact must be made with your child to steal their personal information, thieves will use one of two avenues. The first is to use another child to get the information. Children will tell other children almost anything; that is, unless parents teach their children not to release personal information. For example, a thief who has a child who is residing in the United States illegally, and wants to legalize them in the eyes of the law, or just needs to get them medical care using your child's name, will simply have their child befriend your child to obtain their name, date of birth, and address.

If your child does not have a Social Security number, a thief just needs to obtain or forge a birth certificate or other documents, such as an adoption decree; doctor, clinic, or hospital record; religious record (baptismal record); day care center or school record; or a school identification card. Once they have this information, the thief can submit it to the Social Security Administration to obtain a Social Security card. The Social Security card is issued and sent in your child's name to the thief's address. Once the Social Security card is received, they have all they need to gain access to credit, credit cards, and major purchases.

The second avenue of personal contact involves obtaining a "trusted" position that gives a thief access to children's information. Trusted positions are ones in which a child trusts the person because they are taught to go to him or her for help or questions. Some of these positions might include educators, ministers, first responders, coaches, and medical professionals.

There are other trusted positions that are not as directly accessible to children's information, but they still provide access to children. These jobs might be found at a school, medical provider, day care provider, sports provider, or youth organization. The positions might include, to name a few, a school janitor, school cafeteria worker, medical office worker, medical office cleaning crew, day care worker, day care cleaning crew, youth organization worker, such as a church youth leader, scout group leader, bus driver, or recreational sports leader.

The potential list of who might steal a child's identity is exhausting. It is limited only by your imagination. A parent's job is to educate his or her child on the risks of releasing personal information, and to check credit once a year to ensure the child is not being victimized.

QUESTION #6: IS IT TRUE THAT CHILDREN SOMETIMES HAVE THEIR IDENTITIES STOLEN BY PARENTS OR OTHER RELATIVES?

At the age of seven, Brandon watched as his mother was hand-cuffed and taken away by the local sheriff. Brandon's mother was arrested for using Brandon's identity to secure a job and evade her criminal record. How did she do it? It was quite simple; Brandon's mother falsely used her son's Social Security number when she filled out her job application. This fraud continued for almost a year. It wasn't just a mother trying to support her family; she was intentionally seeking a position that involved access to sensitive billing information—a position similar to one that she used in the past to commit fraud and forgery, which resulted in her criminal record.

—From *Stolen Futures: A Snapshot on Child Identity Theft*[10]

Sadly enough, a significant number of child identity thefts are perpetrated by relatives; often parents. In this question, we will explain how and why relatives steal identities, and how a weak economy is leading some parents to make an ill-advised decision to "borrow" their child's Social Security number to pay bills and other expenses. As you read further, I cover the emotional trauma the child experiences as the result of acts of identity theft by a relative, and its devastating effects.

Those who are not familiar with the crime of child identity theft might ask why a parent would steal their own child's information. Parents who consider themselves in an economic "bind" see little wrong with "borrowing" a child's name to get through a temporary period of financial hardship. This usually begins with the parent rationalizing the crime by saying that it will be temporary and done in part to care for the child, such as regaining a power utility connection that has been cut off.

As with most crimes that initially go undetected, the temptation to do it again proves to be too great, and its frequency increases. This usually leads those using their child's identity to branch out from utility services to non-vital services, such as cable television, additional cable packages, Internet services, or luxury credit items that have little to nothing to do with the care of the child from whom they stole the identity.

Regardless of the reason, parents, relatives, and friends who use a child's information to obtain goods or services are breaking the law. These individuals subject themselves to additional hardships when creditors discover the crime and turn the complaint over to law enforcement. They also subject the child to undeserved emotional trauma when the child discovers the crime.

Seldom does a relative look beyond today or tomorrow when they steal an identity. If he or she did, they would see that they may face both guilt and depression as a parent or relative who has caused emotional damage to someone they are supposed to care for and protect. At this stage, the damage has been done, and trust has been violated.

When a young adult turns eighteen years old and discovers that he or she has been victimized, the journey to repairing their name usually leads the victim to the credit reporting agency. Unsuspecting victims call to report the identity theft problem, wanting the damaged credit history repaired with punishment for the person who committed the crime. As the true details emerge, the victim may discover that the thief was a family member, relative, or friend. At this point, victims usually change their mind, wanting the credit history fixed but without law enforcement involvement.

The financial world doesn't work like that. Agencies are not going to resolve your credit troubles without a police report to verify your claim. You will be left with a personal dilemma of reporting a parent or family member, or living with destroyed credit, unable to buy a home or vehicle, gain employment or college admission, or obtain other needed credit.

Is it true that parents and relatives steal children's identities? Absolutely it is! After all, who knows the personal information of a child better than the child's parent who not only gave the child his or her birth name, but also provided emotional and financial support? My advice to anyone who finds himself or herself facing hard times is to seek public assistance avenues, or to ask extended family for financial help, as opposed to choosing the unlawful act of stealing the identity of a child. Creating hardships for your children is not the answer. If children are our future, then let's give them a fighting chance.

QUESTION #7: WHAT ARE THE MAIN REASONS PEOPLE STEAL CHILDREN'S IDENTITIES?

In the world of identity theft, the types of criminals can be categorized as those who abuse someone's existing account, or those who seek to establish a new account for fraud purposes. Most child-identity-theft-related crimes involve criminals who steal identity information to establish new credit for purchasing power. It may be used to buy goods or services, get credit, obtain a credit card or mortgage, open a checking account, or obtain benefits. Below is an expanded list of items criminals are stealing, and what they are doing with them:

- Cell phone contracts—Thieves love to use someone else's name when obtaining cell phones and smart phones. It opens up a world of communication not previously available to them. Thieves can order items they have no intention to pay for using credit cards they have stolen or obtained falsely. They can organize drug deals, expand criminal activity, or just communicate with friends, family, or even fellow criminals.
- Driver's licenses—Put a criminal's picture on a driver's license and most anyone in the United States would accept it. With a stolen identity, a criminal can become the person whose face appears on the new driver's license. Thieves also commit crimes to raise money for the purchase of ID-making machines. Commercial firms sell ID-making equipment. Criminals can purchase high-dollar equipment and create ID neck-type tags, allowing the criminal to gain access to secure locations. Wallet cards, driver's licenses, and other forms of identification are created from such commercial ID machines, all of which may be fake, but appear real. The ability to get a driver's license, or any official government-recognized identification, is coveted by a criminal.
- Checking or savings accounts—Opening an account with a bank is similar to getting a driver's license in a fake name. Both establish a person as credible. Once a thief writes a check and pays a bill, they establish themselves as a credible customer.

- Bank loans—With a new identity and a clean credit record, a thief can obtain a loan for cash from a bank. Most banks are happy to lend to individuals who have a clean credit history, no bankruptcies, and a good credit score.
- Vehicle purchases—An identity thief can use the clean record of a child to walk into an auto dealership and ride out in a brand new vehicle. This is attractive to a thief, because identity thieves are "all about the flash." New cars, hot cars, flashy wheels, etc., all make the criminal appear more legitimate when he or she moves on to the next scam.
- Electronics purchases—iPods, compact disc players, Wii devices, BlackBerries, video games, car stereos, and any other electronic gadgets that are the rage will be sought after for purchase by identity thieves. While this is just a small list of electronics attractive to thieves, the list is ever-changing with the advancement of technology.
- Department store goods—From clothing and food, to furniture and automotive supplies, the department store is a target for identity thieves. They target department stores due to the variety of merchandise they can get at one location in a short period of time.
- Credit cards—This is the all-time favorite item sought by identity theft criminals. Credit cards generate bills that will not come due for payment for thirty-plus days; thus, a criminal has the freedom to purchase travel, goods, meals, and any other items they desire, charging up the card until they maximize the credit limit.
- Home loans—Most readers would not believe that an individual posing as someone else could obtain a loan significant enough as to purchase a home. It certainly does occur. Call it greed, sloppy loan application procedures, or sometimes having a loan officer as an accomplice to a crime, but it happens every day. The victim, in this case, is not only the individual who had his or her identity stolen, but also the bank and its shareholders.
- Obtaining governmental assistance—Benefits, such as welfare, Social Security, food stamps, and employment compensation, top the list. Thieves are also not above asking for heating assistance in a child's name during colder months, or visiting food banks for food.

- Disaster assistance—After a disaster, many federal, state, and private programs help disaster victims; unfortunately, this is also a call to identity thieves. Thieves will steal a child's identity, or use their own child's information, to obtain assistance designated for those who have suffered from disaster in an area hit by such occurrences as a flood, hurricane, tornado, earthquake, or fire.
- Utility services—Connections such as electricity hookups, water services, natural gas services, telephone services, cable services, and garbage collection are all of interest for an identity thief. This is generally the number-one area that opens the door for parents to the world of child identity theft. A parent feels much less guilty about obtaining a service or good that they feel directly benefits their child.

QUESTION #8: HOW DO TERRORISTS USE A CHILD'S IDENTITY?

There are over 240 valid forms of driver's licenses in the United States with over 10,000 agencies that can issue birth certificates. With so many varieties of identification available, law enforcement is challenged with proving at a first glance that identifications are not valid. It usually requires further investigation by asking questions or doing computerized checks.

A terrorist has a combination of motives for stealing a child's identity. They include financial motives to raise funds, radical motives to advance their cause, and a needed desire to hide their true identity. Terrorists seek and need legitimacy; they want the freedom to move around without question. A few documents that provide the needed legitimacy are a student or employment identification card, driver's license, pilot's license, a vehicle title or lease, mortgage loan documentation, or a passport. All documents listed can be obtained by using a child's stolen information.

Terrorists seek either short-term legitimacy for a one-time operation or a long-period legitimacy, allowing them the freedom to plan for years undetected. A terrorist will stop at little to achieve a desired result. They will commit crimes such as burglaries, home invasions; pickpocketing, and bank robberies. Terrorists will also commit abductions, car break-ins, assaults, threats, computer hacking, gang-related crimes, and other criminal acts to obtain the funds, information, and the access needed or desired.

The 9/11 Commission Report,[11] which was published after the horrific events of September 11, 2001, indicates that terrorists use impersonation as their key tool. The report refers to an Al Qaida training manual that was seized by officials. This manual is now available to the public on the Internet and is used to provide law enforcement officers around the world insight into Al Qaida training techniques. The training manual actually states that trainees are instructed to leave the training camp with five fake, fraudulent, or stolen IDs. These trainees are instructed on how to live off the fake or stolen identities while in the United States or other countries.

Terrorists are the most dangerous and most concerning threats facing law enforcement. They have plans, desires, goals, and organized structure. A child's stolen identity fits their long-term requirement perfectly; providing America with the urgency needed to begin educating parents, teachers, law enforcement professionals, and society on the potential dangers of child identity theft.

Help defeat terrorism by following established guidelines within business and government practices. If you work for an agency that has set a policy of requiring proof of identity by a driver's license, then stick to the policy. Do not accept a library card or other document with just a name that could be easily forged. If you find yourself in a position of authority checking identifications, adhere to your policies. Do not put yourself in the position of accepting a sob story from a con artist. Everyone can make a difference in protecting America.

Lastly, any attempts to obtain documents, credit, or services without proper identity should be reported to the police. Allow the proper authorities to review the information and decide what is suspicious, and what is not. Law enforcement authorities have systems in place to verify identification. Local and state police agencies will report and share suspicious information with the proper federal law enforcement agency in order to piece together a picture of criminal terrorist activity. Terrorists are defeated with the teamwork and vigilance of citizens and law enforcement.

QUESTION #9: HOW CAN MY CHILD'S PERSONAL INFORMATION BE USED BY UNDOCUMENTED WORKERS?

On February 17, 2012, Richmond, Virginia's WWBT NBC 12 posted a story on their website about a Virginia woman who was the mastermind behind an elaborate theft ring.[12] This person bought Social Security cards and Puerto Rican birth certificates from people she knew and sold them to illegal immigrants. Having bought and sold these documents since 2008, she had 50 to 100 legal documents from which to profit. It gets worse. This thief hooked up with a Virginia Department of Motor Vehicles (DMV) employee to enter false information into the motor vehicles system. The thief and the DMV employee were both involved with the issuance of fifty to one hundred valid Virginia driver's licenses for illegal immigrants, all for the sake of profit.

Undocumented workers come to the United States needing documentation to work, receive health care, and buy items on credit. Of these three needs, the public is probably most familiar with the situation of undocumented workers who seek U.S. jobs. Jobs provide for subsistence, items of need, items of luxury, and money to send back to the undocumented worker's family, if they did not come with the individual to the United States.

The Social Security numbers used by undocumented workers are frequently stolen from U.S. citizens, including children. Due to this issue and others involving undocumented workers, federal enforcement agencies have stepped up efforts to check businesses for proof that workers are in the United States legally. The federal enforcement efforts, and the fines that are imposed on businesses who do not comply, have forced potential workers to provide a Social Security number as a condition of employment.

There are many daily examples where children are victimized through identity theft. As previously mentioned, children are fifty-one times more likely to be targeted because an individual in the United States can illegally use the stolen identity for a longer duration without concerns about discovery. Compounding the abuse is the fact that a child's identity is rarely stolen and used one time, but rather most often stolen then sold to multiple illegal undocumented workers.

Child identity theft is perpetuated even further when the stolen Social Security number is used to file tax returns on earned income, on income that was never earned, or to take fraudulent deductions. This creates a nightmare for the child when they file their first return as an adult and find out that they owe the IRS large sums of money, or are the subject of a federal investigation.

Child identity theft can involve undocumented workers using stolen child identities to obtain health care. This health care is for themselves, or themselves and their family. Medical fraud involving stolen identities usually occurs in one of two forms. The first involves health care plans obtained through an undocumented worker's employer using a child's stolen Social Security number when gaining employment.

The second type of health care fraud involves undocumented workers using a child's stolen name, date of birth, insurance information, or Social Security number to obtain medical care, emergency services, prescription drugs, or surgery. Medical fraud involving child identity theft can happen at a doctor's office, clinic, hospital, dental office, orthodontist office, pharmacy, or anywhere medical services are offered or provided. Fraudulent medical care can even take place in a school if the child is enrolled under another child's stolen name.

Regardless of the type of medical fraud, it causes confusion and the possibility that the real child, or the child receiving the care through fraud, will be harmed by the entry of mixed data into the health care medical records system. False data entered into medical records can cause administration of improper medications.

The last reason, of course, that an undocumented worker would desire to steal a child's identity is to obtain credit for credit cards, luxury items, electronics, vehicles, loans, and houses. This makes the undocumented worker no different than the "normal" child identity theft criminal. This individual desires items they cannot afford, or that they can afford but choose not to spend their own money on.

You are best protected from this type of criminal when you keep your child's information safe. Ensure that your child's Social Security card is in a safe place, ask your child not to share their personal information, ask their teachers to be mindful of child identity theft, ask your physician what precautions they take with medical information, and write to a credit agency to see if they have any record of anyone requesting credit using your child's information.

In addition to the steps mentioned above, review your bills closely for medical visits your child did not have; this is a red flag for child identity theft. Review your child's medical records at the doctor's office for conditions they do not have. Lastly, look very carefully at your health care benefits statement for information that tells you that you have reached your benefit plan maximum or limit on benefits. The bottom line is that this should not happen if your child has not had an illness.

QUESTION #10: ARE SOME CHILDREN MORE SUSCEPTIBLE TO TARGETING FOR CHILD IDENTITY THEFT THAN OTHERS?

In the United States, certain children are more likely to have their identities stolen. Categories include foster children, children of Hispanic descent, children in poverty, children with passports, and children known to have good health care coverage. Some children are not in these categories but raise their risk greatly because of their actions or habits.

Foster children and children in poverty are at greater risk because they lack available resources, education on topics of personal finance, and a typical strong, close family support system. These children also lack a consistently safe and secure location to keep valuable documents such as their Social Security card and any insurance documents. While foster children lack consistent parental guidance on issues, children in poverty lack the ability to access money and, therefore, are constantly prioritizing with matters of necessity taking precedence. This means that they might, for instance, need to spend money on food instead of purchasing a safe or lock box to secure important documentation in their home.

The FTC stated in their Identity Theft Survey Report that nonwhites have slightly higher rates of victimization.[13] Children of Hispanic descent who are U.S. citizens are at greater risk due to their proximity to countries with high Hispanic populations. These countries provide the United States with a high number of undocumented workers. Undocumented workers seeking to legitimize look first for someone of their descent. This simplifies the completion of the theft when they go to obtain medical care under the stolen name, or apply for credit in the stolen name.

Children with passports are a target because they have a legitimate document, and the thief must just figure out how to switch the photo and not get caught. Passports are accepted around the world and certainly anywhere ID documentation is required in the United States. The only worry a thief has is ensuring he or she does not present it at U.S. Customs while traveling through our border entry. Computerized scanners will scan the documents and show an alert officer that the photo does not match the person attempting to use the document.

Another category of susceptible children includes those who are known to have very good medical insurance coverage. Children who carry insurance coverage information or personal information have an even larger chance for theft. Types of health care plans, carriers, amounts of coverage, limitations on coverage, deductibles within plans, and benefits are part of the private information that parents must teach children not to release. These documents must be kept in secure locations and accessed only when necessary.

Other factors increase the probability that a child will be targeted for identity theft or crime in general. School systems without strong child identity theft policies put their students at risk. Children who are known to carry sums of cash in their wallet or purse at school increase their chance for identity theft greatly if these items are stolen and their personal information is exposed.

Children who fail to use safe Internet practices expose themselves and their families to identity theft and other harmful crimes. Children who answer unknown text messages or e-mails requesting personal information expose themselves to identity theft and potential physical harm. Many other practices are unsafe and contribute to additional risk.

Are your children at risk? Armed with this information, parents whose children fall into a category mentioned, or who find their children practicing some of the noted unsafe habits, can take steps to increase their security and reduce their vulnerability. Prevention begins with education. Education begins with open and honest discussions between parents and their children.

QUESTION #11: WHAT MAKES FOSTER CHILDREN SO VULNERABLE TO CHILD IDENTITY THEFT?

Foster children are particularly vulnerable to identity theft for reasons beyond their control. These include frequent moves from location to location, as well as frequent placements in temporary homes or facilities. Other factors include the high number of different individuals who have access to the foster child's personal information, lack of education on personal finance, and lack of education on the need for information security. The final factor is critical: the lack of a structured system that understands and institutes identity theft protections for the foster children.

California offers a prime example of foster care troubles. *Newsweek* magazine reported in 2009 that half of the state's 84,000 foster children have been victims of identity theft.[14] This same article detailed how a twenty-year-old man interviewed by the magazine told them he had been victimized when he was twelve years old and did not discover it until he turned eighteen years old. His caretakers had been none other than the state of California foster care system. He has been working for two years trying to clean up his tarnished financial record.

How could California allow this to happen? The issue has become so widespread that the California Office of Privacy Protection commissioned a study titled "A Better Start: Clearing Up Credit Records for California Foster Children."[15] This study, on behalf of 2,110 foster children in Los Angeles County, found that 104 children had 247 separate accounts with an average balance of $1,811 owed. These accounts were opened, on average, when the children were fourteen years old.

In a review of the purchases made through the above abuses, it was found that 74 percent of the accounts were in collection. The most common items purchased with the stolen child identity information were medical accounts, telephone and cell phone accounts, auto loans, and credit card accounts. A mortgage loan was also taken out for the purchase of a $217,000 property. California is but one of the fifty states, and each has its foster care system challenges.

In late 2011, the *Denver Post* published an article about an eighteen-year-old college student who had been a foster child in Colorado.[16] This young adult enrolled in college and set out on her own only to be rejected for credit when she applied for an Internet and cable account through Verizon. The problem was discovered to be a $3,000 debt that she had incurred at the age of eight in the Colorado foster care system.

The problem is overburdened caseworkers, and a lack of priority on finances, while the main priority is on basic needs of the child. Once eighteen years old, a child is emancipated from the system, or "aged out," only to find themselves deep in debt. To add insult to injury, these foster care children have, in some cases, been abused by the caretakers who had control and responsibility for their development and path in life. Imagine turning eighteen years old and having no money to start life with, and little knowledge of how to fix any financial problems.

In September of 2011 President Obama signed into law a requirement that each state run a credit check on foster children who are nearing the age of eighteen years old, and that they assist the children with the cleanup of any discovered identity theft issues. Hopefully, awareness of this issue will only grow and systems will continue to strengthen. If not, then the link between poverty and vulnerability will continue to get worse, and foster children will continue to be disadvantaged from the day they enter the system.

QUESTION #12: WHY ARE HISPANIC CHILDREN IN THE UNITED STATES MORE LIKELY TO HAVE THEIR IDENTITIES STOLEN THAN OTHER CHILDREN?

Child identity thieves are usually motivated by either profit or personal gain. They are of all descents, all races, and both male and female. Child identity thieves participate in child identity theft, medical identity theft, and job- or employment-related child identity theft. Illegal immigrants who work in the United States without proper documentation are considered undocumented workers. Undocumented workers understand that to survive in the United States they must have documents accepted as proof of identity. This documentation must be applied for legally, forged, or stolen.

Undocumented workers, regardless of origin, when seeking to legitimize, look first for someone of their descent. The main reason for seeking someone of their descent is that some identity theft–related transactions must be completed face-to-face. Medical care is a perfect example. Once a thief steals an identity, he or she still must successfully appear in person and present the illegally obtained insurance information and identification to receive the care or prescription.

The United States has historically had a large number of Hispanic undocumented workers who cross the border and seek temporary work in the United States without obtaining proper authorization. Because of this, and the preference to first steal an identity of someone of the same descent, Hispanic children who are U.S. citizens are at a higher risk for child identity theft. These facts are added to the growing knowledge among society that children have financial value, their information is easily obtained, and the duration of theft, undetected, is much longer.

This is not by any means a statement or reference that all child identity thieves are of any single particular descent. On the contrary, child identity thieves are, as previously mentioned, of all races, origins, and genders. The key issue is the need to be legal in order to receive services and employment and to obtain credit.

A trend of concern developing nationally involves identity theft rings obtaining children's stolen information and offering it for sale. These theft rings specifically target children of Hispanic descent who are U.S. citizens. Theft rings desire to cater to the needs of Hispanic undocumented workers, and thus they target Hispanic children to steal their information and sell it to undocumented workers.

Undocumented workers use stolen information to gain employment and health care and often resell the information to others. Those who purchase children's information from theft rings often do so only for the Social Security number. A stolen Social Security number is often presented to an employer coupled with the undocumented worker's real name.

According to the Center for Immigration Studies, "in Arizona 33 percent of all identity theft is job related . . . in Texas it is 27 percent . . . in New Mexico, 23 percent, in Colorado 22 percent, California 20 percent and in Nevada 18 percent."[17] The center maintains that "children are prime targets. In Arizona, it is estimated that over one million children are victims of identity theft. In Utah 1,626 companies were found to be paying wages to the SSN's of children on public assistance under the age of 13."[18]

Identity theft that victimizes children is a serious crime. It is clear that not only are all children at risk, but certain groups of children are at higher risk because of their descent. Reducing this crime is a great challenge for law enforcement now and will continue to be in the future.

QUESTION #13: WHAT ARE "SYNTHETIC" IDENTITY THEFT AND IDENTITY MANIPULATION?

The newest type of child identity theft being experienced and reported to law enforcement is called synthetic child identity theft. The word *synthetic* is actually a derivative of *synthesis*. Synthesis means to take from a combination of sources. Synthetic child identity theft is actually a blend of several different types of identity theft. There are two different methods of committing synthetic child identity theft and a third trend referred to as child identity manipulation.

The first method involves a thief who successfully steals pieces of your child's identity from different sources. If they sift through the school's garbage and find one piece of information on your child, they may try the doctor's office for the next. Then they might try a household trash theft next. The goal of the home trash theft is to steal your garbage before you get up in the morning, looking for documents such as insurance benefits statements, bank 1099-INT statements in your child's name, or an old unshredded tax return listing your child's information. Child identity thieves might try a phone call stating they are your insurance company to get any information they lack. They may try an outbound e-mail to you for missing information not easily obtained from documentation they stole. They might even gain knowledge of school employees and convince you they are calling from your child's school. What sounds preposterous at first is easily believed when you understand the complexity and tenacity of child identity theft and the criminals who do it.

The second form of synthetic child identity theft involves stealing a portion of the identity information. For example, the thief may steal only your child's name. The next piece of information may be fictitious, such as a "made-up" Social Security number. Another piece of information such as the date of birth may be taken from a different child altogether; after all, credit agencies have no records for children, so they have no avenue to verify it. The advantage of stealing partial information is that the thief can take what is easily obtained to create the identity of a new individual, without much further effort than simply creating one piece of information. An example would be a thief who engages a child to obtain his or her name and birthday, but may have no idea what their Social Security number is. A thief using synthetic child identity theft could then create a fictitious Social Security number, add it to the accurate information available, and apply for credit in the child victim's name.

A thief may apply the results of synthetic child identity theft to obtain a fake driver's license and open a checking account. Then the thief can take the driver's license and open a utility account or a cable/Internet account, or even create a fraudulent employment application to get a job.

Synthetic child identity theft can affect several children at once. Schools, doctor's offices, and libraries provide a thief with a one-stop shop for children's information. Identity thieves desiring to participate in synthetic identity theft instead of identity theft against just one child can get multitudes of information by breaking into a pediatrician's office. Once there, they can steal the confidential information of many children and piece them together, mixing the data in an attempt to confuse law enforcement.

Identity manipulation occurs when someone steals your child's information only to change a small piece of information to throw off law enforcement and businesses. Manipulating personal information essentially gives a thief a brand-new identity since most computer systems operate on "exact" matches. An example of child identity manipulation might be to invert the last two digits in the Social Security number and maintain the real date of birth, name, and address. A thief might also submit every detail of your child's identity but change the date of birth by one day, or the year by one year. To accomplish this, the thief needs all the data.

Medical records and school records provide a single source for a data theft, as does purchasing the information from someone who is a relative or friend of your family.

Synthetic identity theft and identity manipulation, both used to defraud children, harm businesses and families. These crimes are the newest trend and will probably mutate further to avoid law enforcement. Our chances for exposing people who commit this crime depend upon the systems of checks and balances we put into place to expose incorrect Social Security numbers and the amount of time law enforcement commits to educating the public on child identity theft crime.

QUESTION #14: WHY ARE CHILDREN WITH PASSPORTS AT RISK?

Children with passports have two things identity thieves want—pristine Social Security numbers and a document that allows them to travel across borders. Your highest risk for theft is when traveling on international flights or boarding international ships where a thief knows you must possess a passport for all family members, including your children. This risk includes your time in the airport or seaport, beginning with your first presentation to a ticket agent.

Your passport documents can be seen by other travelers close to you when you present them, and heard by those close enough to hear. When an airline or ship ticket agent asks for identification, the best course of action is to simply find and present the documents without stating out loud what you are giving to the agent. If the agent requests a verbal response to confirm your identity, use a piece of paper and write it down. It may seem a bit odd, but let the agent know that you are concerned with identity theft and child identity theft.

If you have a passport at home for your child, you should keep it in a safe container. The best place for such a document is a safety deposit box at a bank. If you keep it at home, you should buy a fireproof container with a key or combination lock. If you buy a container with a combination lock, then ensure you use a number that is not your birth date, telephone number, or street address number. Lastly, this container should be kept in your home in a place to which only you, as the parent, have access.

A stolen or lost passport should be reported as soon as possible. To report a stolen passport, obtain a U.S. Department of State Form DS-64 online or from a passport acceptance facility, such as a U.S. Post Office or court clerk's office. I would recommend calling ahead to ensure that the facility you have chosen handles passports.

If your passport is stolen or lost, you must reapply for a new one. You must submit the DS-64 form, which is actually titled "Statement Regarding a Lost or Stolen Passport," with your new passport application. Upon receipt of your application and DS-64 form, the U.S. Department of State will flag your old passport in their computer system and detain anyone using it to try to enter or exit the United States.

When applying for a new passport for your child, all normal stated protocols will apply. There are no shortcuts due to your mishap. The U.S. Department of State requires proof of citizenship. Most juveniles are not old enough to possess a driver's license; thus, there are accepted alternate proofs of identification. The acceptance facility will require several alternates if you do not have a driver's license, so be prepared.

A partial list of accepted alternate proof-of-identity documents is:

- Birth certificate
- Previous passports
- Official military IDs
- Grammar school diploma
- High school diploma
- Baptismal certificate
- Confirmation certificate
- Welfare card
- Student ID cards

For more information on reporting stolen or lost passports, visit www .travel.state.gov. To contact the U.S. Department of State by mail, you may write to them at U.S. Department of State, Passport Services, Consular/ Stolen Passport Section, Attn: CLASP, 111 19th Street NW, Suite 500, Washington, D.C., 20036, or phone at (202) 955-0430.

QUESTION #15: WHY IS EARLY DETECTION SO IMPORTANT?

Two significant problems compound child identity theft. The first is the fact that seldom do thieves steal a child's identity and use it only once. The second problem is that rarely do most people even think of checking their own credit report, let alone their child's. These two issues, coupled with many other contributing factors, spell potential disaster for your child.

Early detection is not just important, it is critical. The longer a thief is able to use your child's identifying information, the more opportunities he or she has to run up debts in your child's name. The FTC states[19] that the top 5 percent of victims spend an estimated 1,200 hours trying to report and correct identity theft victimization. Simply put, early detection and quick action reduce fraud's impact.

An adult's worst worry is that their bank account will be drained. Fraud's impact upon a child is viewed in the worst-case scenario, which is that the identity of your child will be stolen at birth, and it will not be discovered for eighteen years. The path the child's identity will take depends upon the thief who steals it.

What will the journey of your child's name be? Will it be used for terrorism? Will it buy a thief a home? Will your child's information provide medical care for someone in the United States illegally? Will it be used by multiple undocumented workers to gain employment as your child? Will your child be cloned? The path depends upon the thief, but as a parent you can detect the theft early, minimize the harm, and stop the thief in their tracks.

You have taken the first step in prevention and early detection by purchasing this book. Education is the most powerful tool against child identity theft. Someone desiring to victimize your child might attack from many avenues. Prevention and early detection are the best mechanisms to fight this crime. The best place to start teaching prevention and early detection is with families, schools, and the community.

The first step in prevention is teaching your child and family about child identity theft so he or she can protect valuable information. Teaching children about early detection makes them a part of the team of those noticing identity theft clues. A good starting point is obtaining a free credit report for your child, reviewing their computer procedures, reviewing safe texting and cell phone procedures, and teaching them that it is okay to say no to the release of personal information. The last step is working with the community to defeat this crime against children.

Beginning is simple: for the next thirty days, tell yourself that you are going to notice personal information red flags. Does your doctor's office ask you for personal and medical information where others can hear it? Does your child's classroom have information about them posted on the wall? Does your child's teacher lock up student information records they keep? Does your school do background checks on custodian personnel?

What protection does your community provide children? Do you insist on safeguards for foster children? Does your police department have someone trained and assigned to child identity theft crimes? Do you encourage your legislative representatives to address and strengthen laws protecting children from financial ruin?

Early detection involves knowing what to look for. It is important because, if victimized, your children will face emotional trauma. Early detection of child identity theft involving their medical information could save their life. Lastly, early detection will help law enforcement officers track the criminals down and possibly prevent others from being victimized.

QUESTION #16: WHY DOES IT OFTEN TAKE SO LONG TO DISCOVER THAT A CHILD'S IDENTITY HAS BEEN STOLEN?

Parents are often slow to discover that their child's identity has been stolen for a variety of reasons. The primary one is that many people aren't aware of this crime, so they fail to heed the signs that something has gone wrong. Only when the child turns eighteen years old and attempts to get a student loan, a credit card, or a car does the young adult usually discover that years of theft and abuse have ruined his or her credit.

Society is a mechanism of notification for adults. In the eyes of society, children, on the other hand, exist through their parents. If a child owed a bill, the parent would be viewed as the responsible party. The common practice for businesses is to operate on a thirty-day billing cycle. Each month, adults who have revolving credit accounts receive bills for account transactions that occurred during the last cycle. This billing system is how most adults find out that they have been victimized by identity theft.

Children are usually victimized by someone who diverts the address away from the child's actual home address, so discovery of the crime is much more difficult. It usually happens in one of two ways. The majority of discoveries that happen during childhood involve a law enforcement officer showing up at the parent's home with a court-involved collection notice or a warrant for the arrest of the child, who allegedly committed a crime. If the crime is not discovered during childhood, the shock is delivered upon the first credit check done for employment or a loan of any type.

It takes so long to see the signs of child identity theft because we fail to institute protective family policies and ignore the red-flag clues. Detection does not have to wait until disaster. Be proactive in your child's protection. Make it a habit to request your child's free credit report each year around January 1, so you will remember. Discuss with your child's school administration, teacher, and parent-teacher association your concerns about child identity theft. Request that a police crime prevention officer come to your school to educate both parents and teachers on the crime.

Talk with your doctor about medical office practices. How do they secure your child's information? Who has access to your child's information? Do they do background checks on employees? Who cleans their office building? Do they shred all discarded documents? Lastly, ask the doctor what computer security mechanisms they have in place to protect your child's information in their computers.

Child identity theft prevention in your home begins with honest and open discussions about the crime and what children and family members should, and should not, discuss about their personal information. The next step in shortening your discovery time is to put home safeguard steps in place. These include examining all mail and bills closely for irregularities, as well as flagging all children's mail for examination of source by a parent.

Good home policies include ensuring all computers have virus, spyware, and malware detection programs installed. A strong defense would include instituting home shredding policies for documents being thrown in the trash, as well as developing family procedures on depositing mail in a locked mailbox instead of the typical home mailbox.

Once you have put these steps into place, look for the signs that something is wrong. Does your child have a virus on their computer? Are they getting increased daily mail? Are you getting phone calls from businesses, organizations, or people asking for your child? Is your child coming home with a story about someone asking about their personal information? Is there an item on a medical benefits statement for your child that you feel is not appropriate? These are but a few good ways to decrease the amount of time your child will be a victim.

QUESTION #17: WHAT ARE THE LAWS REGARDING IDENTITY THEFT?

When it comes to child identity theft, the law is on your side. The Identity Theft and Assumption Deterrence Act of 1998 made identity theft a federal crime. The 1998 law was strengthened by the Identity Theft Penalty Enhancement Act in 2004, which established a two-year mandatory-minimum sentence that criminals must serve if convicted of aggravated identity theft. This act also provided for a five-year sentence for acts that deal with terrorism

Under federal criminal law, the definition of identity theft is "knowingly transfers, possesses or uses, without lawful authority, a means of identification of another person with the intent to commit, or to aid or abet, or in connection with, any unlawful activity that constitutes a violation of federal law, or that constitutes a felony under any applicable state or local law."[20]

A violation of federal laws can be investigated by any federal law enforcement agency. Identity theft is most commonly investigated by the U.S. Postal Service, U.S. Secret Service, Federal Bureau of Investigation, the Department of Justice, and the Social Security Administration.

In addition to federal laws, each state has a law that addresses identity theft. Table 1.1 shows a list of each state and the corresponding code or statute.[21] You can research your state laws on the Internet by using a search engine and typing in the codes or statutes I have provided. For questions on a specific state code, contact your local prosecuting attorney, commonwealth's attorney, or state attorney general's office.

Table 1.1. State Identity Theft Laws

STATE	STATUTE or CODE
Alabama	Alabama Code § 13A-8-192
Alaska	Alaska Statute § 11.46.565
	Alaska Statute § 11.46.570
Arizona	Arizona Rev. Statute § 13-2008
Arkansas	Arkansas Code Ann. § 5-37-227
California	California Penal Code § 530.5-8
Colorado	Colorado Rev. Statute § 18-5-902
Connecticut	Connecticut Statute § 53a-129 (Criminal)
Delaware	Delaware Code Ann. Tit.5 § 854
District of Columbia	D.C. Official Code § 22-3227.02
	D.C. Official Code § 22-3227.03
	D.C. Official Code § 22-327.04
Florida	Florida Statute Ann. § 817.568
Georgia	Georgia Code Ann. § 16-9-120 through 128
Guam	9 Guam Code Ann. § 46.80
Hawaii	Hawaii Rev. Statute § 708-839.6
	Hawaii Rev. Statute § 708-839.7
	Hawaii Rev. Statute § 708-839.8
Idaho	Idaho Code § 18-3126 (Criminal)
Illinois	720 Illinois Comp. Statute 5/16G-13
Indiana	Indiana Code § 35-43-5-3.5
Iowa	Iowa Code § 715A.8 (Criminal)
Kansas	Kansas Statute Ann. § 21-4018
Kentucky	Kentucky Rev. Statute Ann. § 514.160
Louisiana	Louisiana Rev. Statute Ann. § 14:67.16
Maine	Maine Rev. Statute Ann. Tit. 17-A §905-A
Maryland	Maryland Code Ann. Article 27 § 231
Massachusetts	Massachusetts General Laws § 397-37E
Michigan	Michigan Comp. Laws § 445.65
Minnesota	Minnesota Statute Ann. § 609.527
Mississippi	Mississippi Code Ann. § 97-19-85
Missouri	Missouri Rev. Statute § 570.223
Montana	Montana Code Ann. § 45-6-332
Nebraska	Nebraska Rev. Statute § 28-608
	Nebraska Rev. Statute § 28-620
Nevada	Nevada Rev. Statute § 205.464
	Nevada Rev. Statute § 205.465
New Hampshire	New Hampshire Rev. Statute Ann. § 638:26
New Jersey	New Jersey Statute Ann. § 2C:21-17
New Mexico	New Mexico Statute Ann. § 30-16-24.1
New York	New York CLS Penal § 190.77 – 190.84
North Carolina	North Carolina General Statute § 14-113.20-23
North Dakota	North Dakota Criminal Code § 12.1-23-11

STATE	STATUTE or CODE
Ohio	Ohio Rev. Code Ann. § 2913.49
Oklahoma	Oklahoma Statute tit. 21 § 1533.1
Oregon	Oregon Rev. Statute § 165.800
Pennsylvania	18 Pennsylvania Cons. Statute § 4120
Rhode Island	R.I. General Laws § 11-49.1 – 1-4
South Carolina	S.C. Code Ann. § 16-13-510-530
South Dakota	S.D. Codified Laws § 22-30A-3.1
Tennessee	TCA § 39-14-150 (Criminal)
	TCA § 47-18-2101 (Civil)
	TCA § 47-18-2102 (Civil)
	TCA § 47-18-2103 (Civil)
	TCA § 47-18-2105 (Civil)
Texas	Texas Penal Code § 32.51
Utah	Utah Code Ann. § 76-6-1101
	Utah Code Ann. § 76-6-1102
	Utah Code Ann. § 76-6-1103
	Utah Code Ann. § 76-6-1104
Vermont	Vermont Code § 13.2030
Virginia	Virginia Code Ann. § 18.2-186.3
Washington	Washington Rev. Code § 9.35.020
West Virginia	W.Va. Code § 61-3-54
Wisconsin	Wisconsin Statute § 943.201
U.S. Territories	Do not have a specific law
U.S. Virgin Islands	14 VI Code Ann. §§ 3003
Puerto Rico	Does not have a specific law

2

RECOGNIZING HOW CHILD IDENTITY THEFT HAPPENS

In this section, the author discusses how child identity theft has become so prevalent, detailing how thieves work and common scams they use to extract valuable information from unsuspecting children and their parents.

QUESTION #18: WHAT IS THE PRIMARY WAY CHILDREN'S IDENTITIES ARE STOLEN?

If you are like most parents, you will do anything and everything possible to protect your child. The majority of children's identities, however, are not stolen as much as they are given away. The primary reason children's identities are stolen has to do with a two-part system failure. First, parents fail to be proactive in protecting their children's information, and second, the community has not yet recognized the dangerous effects child identity theft has on children.

If you don't believe me, just ask yourself how many times you've filled out forms with your child's name, birth date, and Social Security number since he or she was born. Now, can you tell me where all those forms are today? Consider this question: how difficult is it to steal information from a child when all the thief wants to know is their name, age, and birthday? What elementary school child does not proudly divulge this information almost on request? The reality is that children's identities are being lost in great numbers each day, in part, because criminals seem to be more aware than parents of the value and accessibility of a child's identifying information. Take again the example of forms you complete about your children: are they shredded as soon as the information has served its purpose? More likely, these documents sit somewhere on a table or a desk visible to anyone passing by. Others find their way to an unsecured file cabinet or a drawer. Your child's medical records likely reside in the records-filing shelf you see multiple employees go to each time you visit the doctor's office.

Left unsecure, your child's identity is not only open to repeat and easy abuse by hardened thieves and terrorists, it is also fair game for opportunistic thieves who find it is much easier to steal information than to pay for the luxuries they want. Take Sarah, a child whose identity was stolen when she was just three years old. She did not find out until years later when she applied for credit on her own and was turned down because thieves had run up more than $500,000 in fraudulent loans and charges in her name. Her parents had no idea how the theft occurred. In small children, however, it usually happens because parents shared the child's information with someone they mistakenly trusted or put it on a form that someone found in an office somewhere and chose to steal it for a new identity.

The good news is that knowledge is power. If you know thieves are actively looking for your child's information, you can make it difficult for them to get. The analogy I like to use is locking your front door. When I was a child, we often left the house by pulling the door shut with never a care that it wasn't locked. We did this because we knew every neighbor and proactively looked out for each other.

Life today is much different. You may live next to someone you do not meet for months, only to learn they are registered as a sex offender. You cannot leave your home unlocked today, regardless of where you live. The same is true for personal information. A Social Security number is not only identification in today's world, but a form of currency that can be converted into cold hard cash, luxury goods, or mountains of debt by unscrupulous individuals. When you fail to be proactive in educating and protecting your children, you are actually "leaving the door open" to your home while they sleep.

How can you make a difference? The first step is to limit what you put on forms you fill out for your children. Most organizations have no need for a child's Social Security number. The second is to sit down with your children and explain to them what constitutes "personal" information. Help them understand to whom it is okay to give their personal information and that it is alright to say "no" to those who ask for their personal information, even if they are adults. Remember, the primary way thieves obtain a child's information is the parent or child gives it away unintentionally.

QUESTION #19: WHAT IS CLONING, AND HOW DO CLONING THIEVES STEAL A CHILD'S IDENTITY?

I remember a movie released years ago in which an individual figured out a way to scientifically "clone," or duplicate, himself. It was a good movie and enjoyable to watch, but imagine that actually happening, without your permission. This is a prime example of identity theft cloning. Cloning is duplicating. Identity theft cloning means your child's identity is permanently stolen, and it is used for criminal and financial gain.

Identity cloning is the most powerful, destructive, and dangerous kind of child identity theft known in society. It does the most harm, has the deepest impact, and is the hardest to recover from. Cloning is calculated and evil.

Identity cloning is a criminal act in which an individual steals your child's life history, and uses that information to establish a new identity in your child's name. This form of cloning is primarily carried out by sophisticated criminals, not for a quick, one-time credit card purchase, or to re-establish utility accounts, but rather for an extended period of time, or forever.

Identity cloning criminals may seek to assume your child's identity because they are planning a crime, or attempting to avoid law enforcement or prosecution. Cloners may be illegal aliens in the United States without proper documentation, or they may be terrorists.

The terrorist wants to clone, not borrow, your child's identity. A terrorist seeking to clone intends to cause your child harm. They are not concerned with the latest iPods, fancy clothes, or the latest trends of fashion; they intend to inflict harm in the name of the cause they believe in. This is not to say that they do not steal or possess expensive things, but their motive is harm, not personal gain. A cloning criminal does not care about the impact identity theft will have on your child. The theft is a necessary step in achieving their desired goal.

A cloning criminal is emotionally detached from the act of identity theft, as well as from the victim. One method of cloning is to target the obituary section of a newspaper. The criminal reads for intelligence, not pleasure. Most obituaries provide the name, date of birth, and date of death of a deceased individual. Experienced child identity thieves prefer to target infant children who are deceased, as it is more unlikely that parents applied for a Social Security number so early in a child's life. Child identity thieves will take the information and apply for a Social Security number, knowing that parents of a deceased child will never have a reason to order an annual credit report.

As if the theft of a deceased child's information is not despicable enough, consider this: if the criminal misses the obituary, a simple visit to the child's grave provides the thief with similar information, such as child's full name, date of birth, and date of death. A reliable national registry protecting children does not currently exist, so our children's information is available to the general public for anyone to steal. My message is simple: with the death of a child, his or her identity may live on if stolen by an identity thief. Parents must still be vigilant in protecting their child beyond death.

Another method for this crime involves an individual seeking out employment opportunities at a school in order to gain access to information on children. While extensive background checks are completed on teachers and administrators, in most educational jurisdictions, less extensive background checks are completed on custodians and cafeteria workers. All a thief needs is legitimate access to the school, and these positions allow more frequent access to schools in odd hours, such as before and after school, and on the weekends. This is absolutely not to imply that all custodians and cafeteria workers are thieves, but rather to demonstrate one such example of how reduced background checks for all those who come into contact with our children may put their identity more at risk to be stolen.

Do not think that it is only our school systems that have such a breakdown. Hotel housekeepers, home cleaning service workers, medical office janitors, and day care janitors are just a few more examples of positions in which thieves seek out reduced background checks in order to position themselves closer to the private information of our children. These occupations require few background checks, yet they have a wide range of access to information.

We are all raised to believe that our first responders are to be trusted. As I mentioned earlier, a child identity thief is emotionally detached from his or her victim. For this reason, the last method I will cover is one I find personally disturbing. The thief may gain employment in a "trusted" position, such as law enforcement, in a fire department, or as part of a rescue unit. While these positions are not as common in identity theft, all the criminal really needs is a uniform suited to a "trusted" profession. The uniform signals to children that it is okay to trust the individual asking personal questions. Children will be more apt to give their personal information to someone in uniform, rendering it more difficult to explain to your child why it is okay to trust a uniformed adult again after his or her identity is stolen.

QUESTION #20: ARE THERE ANY PROTECTIONS AGAINST CLONING?

There are best practices, and preventive measures, to protect your child against cloning. Security professionals use the term "hardening the target." This means that you educate yourself and your family about child identity theft first, and then you proactively put protective measures in place. Once you have family protective measures in place, you should talk to other people, businesses, providers, and organizations to encourage them to do the same.

Previously covered is the fact that both state and federal laws are in place to cover child identity theft, identity theft, and aggravated identity theft. The federal government has identified the Federal Trade Commission (FTC) as the lead agency for collecting identity data, and assisting citizens with reporting identity theft and child identity theft problems. For more information on the responsibilities of, and available assistance from, the FTC, visit www.ftc.gov.

The Social Security Administration (SSA) maintains what is called the Death Master File (DMF). This computerized database is designed to be a federal repository for all death information. Theoretically, the name of every person who dies should be reported to the SSA and listed in the publicly accessible DMF. If all deaths were entered into this file, and done so properly, the file would be a great tool for credit agencies to obtain information from in order to properly consider credit applications, possibly catching a thief attempting to use the information of a deceased individual.

The SSA receives information on deaths from family members, funeral homes, postal officials, state and federal agencies, and financial institutions. According to the SSA's Fact Sheet, *Change to the Public Death Master File*, "The Public Death Master File is a file of all deaths reported to SSA from sources other than States, beginning around 1936. It is not a complete file of all deaths and we cannot guarantee the accuracy of the DMF. The absence of a particular person on this file is not proof that the individual is alive. Further, in rare instances it is possible for the record of a person who is not deceased to be included erroneously in the DMF."[1] Mark E. Hill and Ira Rosenwaike wrote an article titled "The Social Security Administration's Death Master File: The Completeness of Death Reporting at Older Ages,"[2] which sheds light on critical information concerning the death of children and the DMF. The research by Hill and Rosenwaike shows that since 1960, the SSA's DMF has never captured more than 42 percent of deaths for those 0 to 24 years of age.

Another critical issue with the DMF is that it only records information on the death of individuals who have been assigned a Social Security number. If an infant, child, or young adult has not been issued a Social Security number, information on his or her death is not stored with the SSA. A thief is able to use the identity of a deceased child to apply to the SSA for a Social Security card. The SSA is unable to track the fraudulent application due to the information of the deceased child not being included in the DMF. Though there are clear concerns with the DMF, credit bureaus do check the information received from an applicant against the DMF. If a credit bureau finds the applicant's name on the DMF, the bureau will advise the creditor(s) of its findings. The question you need to ask yourself, of course, is whether or not the death of your loved one is among the 42 percent of deceased individuals who make it into the DMF.

If your child encounters a criminal savvy in cloning, your child will be best prepared to handle the situation if he or she has been taught to never provide personal information, and to defer the questions to his or her parents. This is easier said than done, but when a child feels uncomfortable, the best policy is to seek a trusted known adult. If this fails, then you should teach your child to come to you as soon as possible and inform you of exactly who was asking questions of him or her, and what information was released. If you have even the slightest suspicion that your child's personal information or identity has been compromised, contact a credit reporting agency immediately, and request that a ninety-day fraud alert be placed on your child's name and personal information.

QUESTION #21: HOW DO TELEPHONE CALLERS AND SCAMS PUT MY CHILD AT RISK?

Anytime your child speaks to a stranger on the phone, there is a danger that he or she will reveal information that can be used by thieves to cause financial or physical harm. Scammers often say they are taking a survey, calling on behalf of a school, or calling from your banking institution. The caller may say that he or she is calling from a government agency, or advising that you have won a contest. There are ways you can reduce the number of phone calls you receive, and decrease your odds that phone call scammers will target your children.

The twenty-first century has brought an influx of high-tech cell phones, high-speed BlackBerries, and smartphones. These are in addition, of course, to our business and household telephone services. The question of when parents allow their children to have cell phones or smartphones is a family decision. Whether you allow your child to have a phone or not, teach your child what information is appropriate, and not appropriate, to release when talking to someone on the phone.

When the phone rings, a con artist may tell your child they could win an iPod for taking a survey. Another may say they are notifying your family that you have won money in a lottery, even though you cannot remember entering. A scammer may even try to sell you something at a price you cannot refuse to ignore because it is "the lowest available," or it "will only last a short time." Do not allow a scammer to convince you, or your child, that it is acceptable to release personal information over the phone for any reason. Teach your children the lesson of life that if the offer seems too good to be true, it is.

Most scam callers call home phones because residential numbers are easiest to obtain. Screening your calls with caller ID is great, but not foolproof, due to vishing, which is explained in the next question. When talking on the phone, remember that you cannot verify to whom you are speaking. Telemarketers calling your phone could be anyone, of any age, gender, or nationality. There is no absolute way to verify who the incoming caller is, or establish, before answering the phone, the reason they are calling. My question for parents is this: if you cannot verify your caller, how could you expect your child to? Protect your child by teaching him or her not to answer the phone when they do not recognize the number displayed on caller ID. Explain to your child why it is not wise to release any personal or family information to strangers on the phone, regardless of who the caller claims to be.

Protection from scammers, and unwanted telemarketers, begins with visiting the government's Do Not Call list at www.donotcall.gov. On this website, a consumer can list his or her telephone numbers for their home, cell phone, BlackBerry, and smartphone. Registration at the Do Not Call website is free, and it provides protection from telemarketers after the number is placed on the list for thirty-one days. Should you receive telemarketing calls after the thirty-one-day period, the same website is your avenue for filing a complaint.

Other mechanisms can help you protect your child and your family from unwanted or threatening phone calls. Two specific methods are "traps" and "traces." Getting these started requires a call to your phone company. A trap can be set on your phone line for two weeks. Traps trace the origin of unwanted calls. The drawback with traps is that you are required to keep a log with the dates and times of each individual call.

A trace requires no logs and will accomplish the same result; however, it is not free. The cost of a trace will vary from one telephone company to another. All you are required to do is dial *57 after receiving the call, and the incoming call is traced. Note, though, that a trace will only work for calls coming from your local phone network area. Once a concerning call is answered, hang up and dial *57. The local phone company is able to capture the caller's information. Though the information cannot be released to you, you may provide written authorization to your phone service provider to release the call information to the proper authorities for investigation. If your child is receiving concerning phone calls, contact your phone service provider for additional information regarding traps and traces.

QUESTION #22: WHY ARE VISHING, SPOOFING, AND SMISHING SO DANGEROUS?

Vishing refers to a method of information-gathering using "voice over Internet protocol" (VoIP). A child identity thief will use a VoIP line on a computer to make a phone call to target and victimize your child; such calls are difficult to trace. I mentioned in a previous question that you cannot fully verify the caller when using a caller ID system, and this is true. Even with caller ID telling you that it is a phone number, such as your child's school, church, or doctor's office, it could be a trick because of vishing.

Coupled with vishing is "spoofing." Spoofing is using a computer program or downloadable cell phone application to intentionally change the display on someone's caller ID or cell phone. A call could be generated across the street or around the world. When using VoIP, it is easy for a thief to represent himself or herself as legitimate and "spoof," or intentionally change, the caller ID to say they are someone else, a business, or a government entity (i.e., social services, a utility company, your local school, a department store, the police department, a federal agency, etc.).

Absolutely anyone can spoof. Anyone online can access the fee-based system and pay to spoof a call. Websites such as www.spoofcard.com and www.spooftel.com allow you to buy spoofing minutes to spoof your friends, family, or anyone you desire. You can spoof a home phone or cell phone. Spooftel even advertises that you can share your minutes with your Facebook friends.

In addition to vishing and spoofing, there is "smishing." Smishing, according to the Federal Bureau of Investigation (FBI) website, is a combination of SMS (short message service) texting and phishing. The example provided by the FBI is someone texting you saying that they are your bank and advising that there is a problem with your account. The text provides a telephone number for you to call. When you call the number and provide the required security number, the thief drains your account. Children can be fooled the same way. Thieves can text children stating they are from the cell phone company and need a return call to verify personal information in order to keep the phone from being disconnected We must teach our children not to reply to such requests for information, as the thief is playing on their fear; if I do not call back, my phone will be cut off.

Other sites go even further. SpoofAPP (www.spoofapp.com) allows you to spoof from your cell phone. Kids with this application can spoof other children, or be spoofed by adult thieves posing as children. SpoofAPP offers you the ability to change your voice to disguise yourself and sound like someone else, which is frightening. An additional application from SpoofAPP allows you to record all calls and play them back later. The bottom line for parents is that you do not know who is calling your child, or what they are doing with the information they are obtaining.

The mechanisms of vishing, smishing, and spoofing are often used in con scams in conjunction with computer random phone dials. In this scam, thieves use "war dialers" to computer call randomly selected telephone or cell phone numbers. It may be programmed as a single call, or the computer may be calling multiple numbers at the same time.

If your child responds to a vishing telephone message, text, or SMS, be prepared for the caller to request detailed personal information from your child for "security" reasons. Why do they do this? Well, before the call or text, your child was an unknown individual randomly selected. Once they answered the phone, or responded to the incoming message, your child became a "mark" or target for identity theft.

Spoofers using vishing and smishing will ask questions such as your child's name, address, date of birth, Social Security number, and possibly even your child's school information. If the spoofer asks for partial information, they may direct you to another department or office, which will actually be another spoofer sitting next to the identity thief. The spoofers work in unison to collect as much information as the child will release. Once the spoofers put it all together, they have your child's entire identity. As you can see, cons and scams have the potential to be complicated even for adults. Imagine being a child in today's society.

QUESTION #23: HOW CAN INFORMATION STOLEN AT AN ATM COMPROMISE MY CHILDREN?

We all know how someone who sees you key your personal identification number (PIN) into an ATM can ultimately steal money from your bank account. Once a thief has your PIN, what does she or he really have except a set of numbers? To complete an illegal transaction, the thief needs your ATM card or the information from your card's magnetic strip. In this question, you will read ways to better protect yourself against theft during a visit at the ATM.

Thieves often target ATMs for robbery. The crime is often viewed as a "holdup" as soon as you get the cash out of the machine. An easier crime for savvy criminals is to watch an ATM for someone who plans to make a "quick visit." As the person hurriedly exits the car, the thief jumps into action, opening the car door and stealing what you have left unsecured within an arm's reach. The majority of the time, it is a purse or wallet containing confidential identity information.

When you discover personal and family items missing, the reality of cleaning up the identity theft mess may escape you. Beyond contacting your credit and bank card companies to advise them of the theft will be an entire new reality that someone has your personal and family information. The most realistic approach to this is to stop what you are currently doing, bookmark this page, and go get your purse or wallet.

When you have your purse or wallet, take out the contents and tell me what you see. Most will have a driver's license, ATM card, credit cards, and membership cards. Nearly everyone has photographs of family. What is as important as the photo on the front is the information usually written on the back. Did you write the child's name and age? If you did, then a thief has your child's name, age, and from your license, your child's address.

Do you carry your child's Social Security card in your wallet? How about their prescription or health care card? Do you have your child's school ID or school photo? All of this is information that child identity thieves desire. It may be hard to believe, but the reality is that you might not have been the target of theft in the first place; it may have been your child's information they were after.

ATM thieves usually vary in their sophistication. The lower end of savvy criminals may "hold you up," while the more intelligent thieves may use ATM card skimmers to simply steal your information as you swipe your card, later to be used to drain your accounts once you leave. Both are a violation of your privacy, and each has repercussions.

Harden yourself and your family as a target. Make the commitment now to go through your purse or wallet and take out those items that identify your family. Carry in your purse or wallet only needed or required items. When you need to visit an ATM, be wise in your selection. Find one that has very good lighting at night and is attached to the bank. Wait in your car until the ATM is free. Once you leave the car, lock the door behind you, preferably with your electronic door key if your car has one. When you complete your ATM transaction and turn to go toward your car, use the electric key button to open the door so you can quickly get into your vehicle. Immediately lock your car door, and leave the bank area. Do not sit in the parking lot to count your money, as you remain a target to a thief.

Lastly, go through your car for any other items that may be considered "identifying" paperwork. Think to yourself, if my car was broken into tonight, what information would thieves get about my family? Child identity theft prevention begins by taking proactive steps to protect you and your family.

QUESTION #24: WHAT IS CHILD-TARGETED PHISHING AND PHARMING?

Imagine you are on a riverbank and want to cast your fishing pole into the water. You have no idea exactly what fish, if any, may lie below. All you want to do is to throw your bait out there and see what bites. If you were using a computer instead of a fishing pole, and your targets were people instead of fish, that would be phishing. But wait: don't some fishermen like saltwater fishing, and others like freshwater fishing? Wouldn't some of the anglers rather fish a lake for bass, while others love the taste of a deep-sea flounder?

Phishing thieves are the same way. Some target adults, while others target children. Some thieves target Internet games and others target e-mails with lottery scams. What is consistent in phishing is that they intend to take from you more than you will receive.

Child identity theft in phishing is when your child is targeted with scam e-mails to get them to respond back with personal information. The e-mail appears to be from a legitimate company. The e-mail often tempts children with free computer games or other enticements if they "register" with personal information. Phishing scams are not designed to give you anything of value, regardless of their claim. Their main goal is to get your personal information, family information, credit information, or bank information.

In addition to phishing is "pharming." Pharming is a computer hacker's attack on a website that redirects traffic to another bogus website. There is also "drive-by pharming." Drive-by pharming uses the JavaScript on a website created by a computer hacker that reconfigures broadband routers. When a child clicks on a link, the hacker's JavaScript changes the Domain Name System (DNS) settings to reconfigure your home's broadband router.

The end result is that the hacker has control over what your child sees or what they believe they see. If the computer is shared, your next session on the computer could have you believing you are going to your bank's website, when in fact you are headed to a fake hacker site that looks like your bank's website. Once you enter your user ID and password, the thief is able to drain all your financial accounts.

Parents should watch for an increase in "pop-ups" on their children's computer. Pop-ups are a sign that the child's computer may have been attacked by hackers who are collecting information from their computer as it runs. These same tech-savvy criminals might be using keystroke collection technology to gain access to all passwords on the computer.

Quite problematic for law enforcement officials are the phishing and pharming scams from foreign countries. Local and state police are powerless in enforcing any laws against people outside the United States, and federal law enforcement agencies have very little authority or power to influence those who do have the enforcement authority in a foreign country. Policing the Internet is difficult, if not impossible.

Several tips to protect your child include the following:

- Never trust a stranger on the computer.
- Never give out personal information over the computer.
- Verify information received via another source, such as a telephone directory.
- Do not fall prey to threats. If you receive threats, contact the police.
- Look for a lock at the bottom right of your web browser, or the "https://" at the beginning of the web address for secure information transmission.
- Look for web addresses that are numbers instead of letters as a red flag.
- Look for grammatical errors.
- Be cautious of offers that are too good to be true, as they usually are.
- Be cautious of friend referrals, as a friend's computer may have been compromised.
- Change your password often with a "hard" password. A hard password is one that is complex, unrelated to easily obtained personal facts about your child, and contains different styles of characters such

as numbers, upper- and lowercase letters, and characters such as *, #, @, !, or ^.

- If you dispose of an old computer, be sure to remove the hard drive, which may contain valuable information about your child.

QUESTION #25: HOW CAN MALWARE ACCESS MY CHILD'S PERSONAL INFORMATION?

In February of 2009, a Chicago man noticed suspicious activity on a bank account he set up for online purchasing. According to an article written by Jennifer Waters for *MarketWatch*,[3] six months later this man had accumulated over $900,000 worth of bills. What is equally disturbing is the fact that the victim has spent over $100,000 of his own money in an effort to clear his name, and clean up his damaged financial history, due entirely to criminal identity theft.

How did this happen? In this case, the thief used malware. Malware, short for malicious software, is a computer malicious code that is stealthily inserted into your computer and "sleeps" until you access pertinent data. Its design is to disrupt your computer, steal information, and gain access to your computer systems. For this victim, the culprit was keystroke malware that recorded him entering his computer and captured the strokes of his password as he accessed his bank account.

The victim mentioned above was no child. He was a sophisticated, very intelligent individual who possessed a doctorate degree, yet he found himself victimized by malware. The point here is that this individual had advanced education, yet thieves still were able to get into his computer and manipulate what he thought was private and protected personal information.

Malware began as an experimental worm prank in early Internet MS-DOS systems. Since its invention, malware has migrated into sophistication. Modern malware may come to you in the form of a virus, worm, or Trojan horse. It can steal your child's information and any information they might have on your family in their computer.

Below are suggestions for what you can do to help prevent a thief from using malware on your child's computer:

- Ensure all computers you use have virus and malware protections.
- If you receive an e-mail from someone you do not know, delete it.
- Use strong privacy settings on your computer.
- Scan your e-mails for viruses with your virus software before you open them.
- If a friend sends you a website link and a strange message or file, delete the e-mail.
- Do not forward chain e-mails.
- Delete all unwanted messages without opening.
- Do not click on advertising you are not familiar with.
- Keep your security patches up to date.

Spyware is another tool that easily enters your computer. Spyware seeks to track your child's preferences on sites they visit, purchases they make, and ads they click on. Spyware does not spread like a virus. It is installed by exploited security holes or packaged with user-installed software, or peer-to-peer applications. Your best protection from spyware is to install a service such as SpyHunter, which can be found at www.enigmasoftware.com.

Does your child have an Android phone? Technolog, on NBCNews .com, conducted a study that found that Android malware is up 400%.[4] Did you know that fifty bad applications, or apps, currently carry malware? According to an article by NBCNews.com titled "Malware infects more than 50 Android apps," users' personal information could be at risk.[5] Before you allow your child to install an app on his or her phone, make sure to check the permission the app is asking for. If the app needs more permission than is required, avoid it. Never install an application package file (APK) on your child's Android phone unless you are absolutely sure it is 100 percent safe. This may require you to research the app to find reviews others have done on the app. Lastly, be cautious of "free" apps, as they may not truly provide the free service the user intends to receive. A free app may contain a virus.

Parents must be involved in their child's computer usage regardless of age. A download from the wrong site may send their child's identity down a path of irrevocable damage. The supervision kids complain about now may save them from financial ruin or physical harm should they encounter a hacker. Is your child prepared to defeat a hacker? Protect yourself, and your child, with education and prevention.

QUESTION #26: WHY DO CHILDREN WHO HAVE GROWN UP WITH RULES AROUND COMPUTERS STILL FALL VICTIM TO SCAMS?

Scams are big business for a small segment of society. Their ability to survive in the identity theft market depends on their success rate in stealing children's identities. If you look closely at child identity thieves, their methods are like mutating viruses. Criminals are always devising new scams because law enforcement officials become aware of their tactics, inform the public, aggressively investigate their crimes, and help the legislative community develop appropriate laws.

This cycle is challenging even for law enforcement agents. They must stay trained on the latest techniques being used, and communicate continuously with other law enforcement agencies. If child identity theft challenges law enforcement professionals, imagine the obstacles for parents who have little education on the crime. If you look hard at this scenario, it would seem that children do not have a chance.

The question one must ask oneself is, where do I begin? We have spent a great deal of time developing computer usage rules in schools and at home. Some rules protect you from a system crash, and some protect you from being physically harmed. The rules that parents, school administrators, and children agree on are easy to enforce. All should easily agree that you must have some type of virus program on your computer to survive.

Children who have grown up with computer rules fall victim to scams because they are not educated on child identity theft, scams, or fraud. Many children believe that they are smarter than their parents, who were not raised in an advanced electronic age, but rather adapted to advanced computer programs, iPods, BlackBerries, texting, and other electronic devices. The truth is that, as parents, the more complex your life, the less time you have to spend on electronic luxury items; therefore, you focus on exactly what you need to do to get through your daily activities, and possibly less time on educating yourself on how to protect your child against identity theft.

Children see handheld electronic games as fun pastimes and entertainment. They view the games as challenging and an expansion of their learning. What they often do not see are the potential dangers associated with computers, gaming, cell phones, SMS, and texting. Parents understand that scams do exist, and offers too good to be true raise red flags. Children, including young adults, need to understand this as well, hopefully to help them avoid falling victim to electronic invasion and theft.

How do you reach your children? By this I mean, how do you impress upon them important messages in life? The best influences in children's lives are their parents and guardians. Children will adhere to what they know you will enforce. They will be receptive to what is best conveyed in a way that they will understand. You know how to reach your child's mind. Talk to them about security protocols. Discuss and reiterate that danger lurks when you let your guard down.

Our children are very smart and will surprise you. Give them the opportunity to come to you with suspicious items they receive. Talk to them as a family to help other family members best comprehend what lurks outside. Share what you have learned from news items and other sources to help battle cyber crime.

Lastly, challenge your local and state police to bring the community the latest education on scams, schemes, cons, and harmful crimes. Mutating crimes are best fought as a community. Child identity theft will only be defeated when we make it unprofitable.

QUESTION #27: WHAT IS A MEDICAL "LOBBY LISTENER," AND HOW CAN THEY HARM MY CHILD?

Those who work in the medical profession deserve a great deal of respect for caring for the sick and injured. They are specialists in their expertise, and they are admired. The medical profession, however, needs help with understanding what child identity theft is and how it affects children. From doctors and dentists, to orthodontists and pharmacists, each needs to be better educated on the aspects of the crime, as well as how their actions could possibly contribute to someone stealing a child's future.

Most, if not all, Americans visit a doctor, dentist, orthodontist, or pharmacist each month only to have the receptionist ask the patient to verbally verify information. Most, if not all, times this is done for everyone in the waiting room to hear. Quite often these offices have clipboards asking you to write down personal information on a check-in sheet left in public view. Want to know a patient's name? Just sit in the waiting room. Trying to guess where they live? No need to—the pharmacy employee may require you to tell them in open questioning. What can a thief do to steal a child's date of birth to get a credit card? Simply sit in the waiting area of any of these service providers.

Health information is stolen each and every day by "lobby listeners" who camp out in the waiting area of a service provider listening for both children and adults to comply with medical requests. Thieves do not need your family policy number when they have your name, address, telephone number, Social Security number, and reason for your visit to a service provider's office. Armed with this information, a thief can call your insurance company, provide the last doctor, dentist, or medical specialist visited, reason for the last visit, and personal identifying information, and the insurance company will provide the thief with the child or adult's identifying medical insurance number.

If you followed a patient through their medical visit, you would notice that identity theft starts with the doctors' offices and continues with the pharmacy. Customers visiting a pharmacy are asked almost all of the same questions that the doctor's office receptionist asked for everyone in the lobby to hear. The difference is that the pharmacy employee will discuss openly with a parent what medication has been prescribed for your child, and the details of how your child should use it. As you wait for your child's prescription to be filled, you may shop for food, cards, laundry detergent, and more, but a thief immediately uses the information he or she overheard to begin the application process for fraudulent credit in your child's name.

It is worth reiterating once again that children are fifty-one times more likely to be victimized. The description above is of just one method. It does not take into account theft from "shoulder surfing," which is the act of a thief looking over someone's shoulder when he or she is working on a computer. It also does not account for theft from within the office by staff, custodian personnel, or after-hours break-ins where files and information are stolen.

So what can we do to help the situation? Parents are definitely the key to information security. In most cases, you can have a direct impact on the security of any medical office you frequent. Advise the medical staff that you are concerned about identity theft and prefer to write down information to answer their questions, unless they allow you to go in a private setting where no one can hear your answers. The more often parents say this to our service providers, the less likely the staff will continue asking private questions in the current format.

Another great suggestion is to talk to your doctor during the visit. Ask your doctor if he or she is aware of child identity theft. Education is the key with child identity theft. If parents, doctors, pharmacists, teachers, and the community understand the crime, then all will certainly take more proactive measures to help protect our children. Success in defeating child identity theft will be found in community awareness and proactive prevention steps.

So let's get started. Next time you are at the office of a service provider for a medical visit, ask to see your child's medical file. They will probably be caught off guard and not want you to take it from the office. That is fine. Just ask to sit in a quiet room and view the file. What are you looking for? Most importantly, you want to look for anything that you did not approve. Are there doctor's visits you did not bring your child in for? Surgery or procedures your child did not have? Changes in your child's blood type, address, or age?

Make the same request of your pharmacy. Get a printed list of all medications that have been issued to your child over the last year. Review the list for unapproved items. Unapproved items are red flags that can not only stop child identity theft, but just may save your child's life.

QUESTION #28: HOW CAN MY CHILD'S SCHOOL INADVERTENTLY JEOPARDIZE PERSONAL DATA?

Teachers are a special class of people. They are great with children, they love their work, and they love to develop young minds. They have the best interests of children in their hearts and minds at all times. Teachers, principals, and school administrators and staff just need education in areas in which they do not specialize, such as crime.

Identity theft education is the responsibility of law enforcement. It is not as easy as you might believe because scams mutate very often to avoid law enforcement. Staying abreast of the latest child identity theft trends is a challenge. Thank goodness easy steps can be taken to help maintain an approach through prevention in our schools to protect children of all ages.

The best approaches to child identity theft prevention are broken down into three categories: elementary school prevention, middle or junior high school prevention, and high school prevention. Each category has its own unique challenges. Younger children are the most vulnerable because of their inability to understand the complexity of child identity theft. It is uniquely challenging to make high school teens believe that the threat is real and can touch each of them through malware and devastating identity theft scams.

Our first challenge is elementary school. This is both the best place to obtain information for thieves, and the best place to start prevention steps for parents, teachers, and law enforcement. I have been proactive in crime prevention for my entire career as a law enforcement officer. The one thing that I recognize as consistent in every elementary school classroom I have been in is the décor of the room, which includes the children's names.

In most all classrooms, teachers write children's names on each of their desks. In some classrooms, teachers post children's birthdays on a wall for celebration. Fun times for the children, right, as your name on the birthday wall means you are probably eating cupcakes on your special day to celebrate. While this might be fun for the children, and a mental break for hardworking teachers, it is child identity theft information for thieves. Take advantage of your next trip to your child's class to see if you recognize security weaknesses, such as this example, and point them out to the teacher.

Middle or junior high school is a step up in responsibility and a taste of what is to come in the years ahead. While children at this age seem to have a grasp of operating computers, they do not understand the complex dangers the computer can bring. Parents and teachers can use this opportunity to start discussions on viruses, worms, and Trojan horses that steal information, and crash computers. This is also the age to advance your discussions on child identity theft and computer predators.

High schools present the greatest challenge. Teachers are shadowing less than in elementary and middle school, and students are expected to be more responsible. By this age, teens think they know more about computers than most parents, because many of their requested gifts center on the latest electronic gadgets on the market.

The truth is that teens are a big target for thieves because they interact more on the computer than any other age group. Teens are more likely to respond to ads or surveys, select free downloads, or interact with social media. Teens are also a big target for sexual predators. Successful approaches must include a partnership between parents, school administrators, and local law enforcement. Schools are definitely a target for child identity thieves regardless of the age group. We must use education and reinforce both the rules for usage and potential computer dangers.

QUESTION #29: WHAT STORY DOES MY OFFICE CUBICLE TELL ABOUT ME AND MY CHILDREN?

What does your office, work space, or cubicle say about the employee and their family? Sit at your desk, or at a coworker's desk, and be objective: tell me what you see. Where did they go to college? What is their favorite sports team? Did they serve in the military? Have they had their picture taken with any celebrities or political figures? Are they married?

More importantly, what does your office say about your children? What sports do they play? Where do they go to school? Where do they vacation? What are the approximate ages of the children? What are the likes and dislikes of the children?

A professional's office is a display of who the individual is and where he or she has been in life. Identity thieves seeking to steal children's identities look beyond the certificates on the wall. They seek family photos and personal information. Whether it is a photo thumb-tacked on a cubicle wall or a photo in a frame, a thief looks at your work area for intelligence.

Using the theory that knowledge is power, what could someone cleaning your office after hours learn about you and your children? If you place notes to yourself in your work space, what do they say? Does your child have a doctor's appointment? Do you need to return a call to their sports coach? Has your child's teacher requested a conference? These questions and others seem harmless, but an identity thief can turn them into intelligence. Identity thieves can return your phone calls to a teacher and pose probing questions for verification.

The next concern is the information you do not lock up after hours in your work space. Your desk, private file drawer, or locker is usually considered a private area where you can keep information and items that only you can access. You may not have an office to lock, but if you do, is it locked when you are away from your desk, when the office is closed, or on days when you are not at work? If the answer is no, then it is accessible to coworkers, service providers, custodians, and visitors when you are not there.

Have you ever worked with a nosy coworker? How about a micromanaging boss? Who can see your computer screen? Who has access to your computer password? Is your password your children's names? Slow down and take the time to make sure your work space is secure.

Here are some tips for protecting your work area:

- Lock your office after hours.
- Request that your office be cleaned during business hours.
- Encourage your business to institute a visitor pass program if you do not have one.
- Do not leave your purse or wallet unsecured at work.
- Limit information about your children in your office.
- Do not store information about your children and family on your computer.
- Wipe all hard drives on old computers turned in to get rid of personal information.
- Do not leave personal U.S. mail on your desk.
- Lock up any flash drives or external hard drives not being used.
- Be observant of anyone who lingers around when you are working on the computer.
- Create computer passwords that are difficult for thieves to figure out.
- Set your computer screen to default to a password when you walk away for any period of time.

- Do not leave your password underneath your mouse pad or keyboard.
- Be mindful of the personal information you put on a calendar in your office.
- Shred all paperwork when discarding it; use a cross-cutting shredder.

QUESTION #30: HOW DOES MAIL THEFT PROVIDE IDENTITY THIEVES WITH VALUABLE INFORMATION?

Stealing your mail can be a bonanza for identity thieves. In addition to credit card numbers, thieves can get their hands on information about bank accounts, insurance, household utilities, credit bills due, names of house occupants, magazines subscribed to, cell phone or home phone bills, records of calls, and more.

Even more important than bills is the knowledge that can be gained about your children. If someone steals your mail today, what you fail to see might not ever be missed: magazines your children subscribe to, offers they might receive, or cards they should be getting. Eventually, you might find out about insurance benefit statements missed, letters mailed from your child's school, bills received in their name, or a birthday card a relative sent that wasn't received.

Mail theft can be passive or aggressive. A passive theft is when someone, such as your letter carrier, newspaper carrier, or anyone depositing something in your mailbox, examines your mail without tampering or opening it. Aggressive theft is when someone steals your mail, opens it, whether covertly or overtly, and examines it. In either case, information is gained about your children and your family.

As important as what mail items you receive is what mail items you send, and how you mail them from your home. I call this the "red flags of easy theft." Imagine yourself driving around from 4 a.m. to 5 a.m. in the morning while people are sound asleep. What do you see? In most neighborhoods, whether urban or rural, you can find multiple mailboxes with their red flags up to notify the postal carrier of mail awaiting pickup. While this was a safe option of mail delivery some time ago, in current day's society of identity theft the red flag screams "OPEN ME AND STEAL MY CONTENTS." The mailbox red flag is great for criminals because they do not have to go house to house looking for items to steal—they just need to stop at the boxes with the flag up.

How do you defeat mailbox theft? The best way is to take your old box down and replace it with a locking-type mailbox. Ensure that what you purchase is approved by the U.S. Postal Service, but do your family a favor and replace it now. This change will prevent those who are not supposed to have access to your mailbox from gaining access and stealing the mailbox contents. If you cannot afford to replace your mailbox, then you need to time your mail deposit or take your mail to a U.S. postal drop-off. Timing your deposit means knowing what time your letter carrier comes by and dropping your mail in the box just before he or she arrives.

The government has recognized that mail theft and identity theft are problems. The U.S. Congress passed a law called the Social Security Number Confidentiality Act of 2000. This law helps with passive identity theft of mail by requiring the secretary of the treasury to ensure that Social Security numbers are not visible through or on unopened mailings the government mails out. Mailings, such as government checks, are now designed so that you cannot see an individual's Social Security number without opening the mail. Now that the government has done their part, have you done yours?

Here are some tips to help prevent mail fraud:

- Never respond to an organization with a postcard containing family information.
- Always deposit mail in a locked mail container or at the post office.
- Get to know your letter carrier and your newspaper deliverer.
- Never leave checks or money orders in your personal mailbox.
- If you vacation, ask the post office to hold your mail.

If you have any reason to suspect that your mail has been stolen or tampered with, contact your local post office and ask them for the contact information of the U.S. postal inspector responsible for your area.

QUESTION #31: WHY WOULD SOMEONE STEAL MY HOUSEHOLD GARBAGE?

I am an avid recycler. Recently, I went to the recycle site run by my county government to drop off my goods. The drop-off site was located in front of a local fire station. They had separate containers for plastic, mixed paper, and newspaper. The newspaper container was a large dumpster. I dropped off the plastic, then dumped my mixed paper and made my way to the newspaper container. As I opened the door to the container, I was startled to see a woman sitting inside, right square in the middle of the container on top of the newspapers.

I assume this dumpster diver was a newspaper coupon collector, but for all I know she may have been in the mixed paper dumpster before she got into the newspapers. In my case, I contacted the county recycling agency to explain the situation. To my surprise, the county agency had no signs posted stating that you could not get into the containers. I could not help but wonder what information in that container was at risk.

What you throw in the trash could be a goldmine to someone looking to steal your family's identity. Documents such as insurance benefit statements, school documents, medical bills, credit card receipts, voided checks, utility bills, tax forms, and family birthday cards are valuable finds for someone looking to steal an identity. Once you dump your trash in a community dumpster, school or office trash can, or take your trash container to the end of your driveway, an army of identity thieves is waiting to go through your refuse for information.

The method of sifting through trash is affectionately referred to as "dumpster diving." It is the process of stealing someone's discarded items and physically sifting through their trash. A criminal might look through your employee trash can at work, go through the trash container outside your child's school, or steal your curbside trash before the trash collector has the opportunity to pick it up. If your first reaction is the feeling that this cannot be legal, you are incorrect. Discarded trash is the property of the person who possesses it. In other words, once you throw it away, you lose the right of privacy concerning the trash items.

Dumpster diving is one of the most overlooked and potentially divulging methods available to identity thieves. Face it, we have all accidentally thrown something in the trash and had to go digging through the nasty garbage looking for an item or piece of paper. Our first reaction is disgust at the thought of going through the trash. To an identity thief, garbage theft is much like digging for gold. They go through your trash seeking that one nugget of information that will bring him or her a rush of excitement.

I know what you are saying to yourself by now upon reading this: garbage theft is one of those things I have heard about, but I do not believe people really do it except in cases of espionage or divorce. I am here to tell you that not only is it real, but it is one of the easiest methods of stealing your information. Remember, you freely put personal trash out for someone to take it away; thus, it doesn't need to be stolen.

Always think "identity theft." When you are at work or on the road, at a fast-food restaurant, at an interstate rest stop, or staying in a hotel or anywhere else you throw something away, think about what it is you have in your hand before discarding it. Always ask yourself what will be known about you or your family if someone finds that trash.

Precautionary measures are your best defense. What precautionary measures have you taken in your household to protect your children before throwing away garbage? Have you properly shredded any and all information that contains personal data? Have you used a clear bag that advertises what is available for the trash collector to be tempted by? If you take your trash to a government-owned dumpster, when is the pickup? Does the trash sit for a week or more, open to those wishing to dig through it?

You control how your family processes your trash. Just remember that once you let it go, it's trash, and now the property of someone else. Protect yourself with good preventive policies regardless of where you may be.

QUESTION #32: WHAT IS THE BEST WAY TO PROTECT DATA ON MY LAPTOP?

Society's fast pace makes us increasingly mobile as a workforce. Unfortunately, this can put our children at risk because of the personal data that family members, businesses, schools, and medical providers store on their laptop computers. Laptop thefts, data breaches, and improperly discarded laptops put our children at risk every day.

Most laptop thefts occur not only for the value of the laptop itself, but for the data that has been stored on it. The *Star Tribune* in Minneapolis, Minnesota, published an article in September of 2011[6] detailing the theft of a laptop computer from a car parked at a restaurant. This computer contained the information of approximately 14,000 patients of a local health care system, and 2,800 patients of a local medical center. Unfortunately for the patients, the data on the computer was not encrypted.

Most readers would think that this type of breach in security is rare. The same article stated that it was the second time in the same year in the twin cities of Minneapolis–Saint Paul that a stolen laptop contained high numbers of victims' personal information. The companies that cause this type of catastrophe can purchase identity theft protection for your family, but the fact still remains that your name, date of birth, Social Security number, and potentially your medical history are out there in someone else's hands.

Laptop computers are a target when left in your vehicle or when you travel through an airport, train station, or by ferry. Laptops are easy thefts when left in taxis, on airport baggage claim conveyor belts, airport security screening areas, at conferences, in hotels, or in rental cars. Laptop size is decreasing to increase their mobility, so they are getting harder to keep up with. The best way to protect data on your laptop is to minimize the personal information you store on it. Forty-two percent of data breaches in the United States occur due to lost or stolen laptops or other data-bearing devices, which is why laptops are targeted by identity thieves.

Beyond minimizing the information you store on your laptop, you must encrypt your data. The Ponemon Institute estimates that the average cost of an employee's lost laptop is $49,246.[7] This price includes the cost of laptop replacement, loss of software, forensics, data breach, and investigation cost. The price also includes the loss of intellectual property rights, legal costs, and employee costs incurred in trying to locate the device.

While we can capture approximate costs of corporate computers, how do you put a price on stolen personal information, such as medical information and photographs? Encryption begins with development of passwords that are not easily guessed by thieves. Never use children's names, pets' names, or dates of significance. Use combinations of numbers, lower-case and upper-case letters, and special characters.

Here are a few tips for protecting your laptop:

- Always keep your laptop physically with you when traveling through an airport, train station, or by another other form of transportation.
- As with any computer, never discard a laptop unless you have wiped the hard drive clean of all personal and business information.
- Ensure all data on your laptop is password protected.
- Report any laptop theft to the police immediately.
- If your laptop is stolen and contains family information, immediately place a ninety-day fraud alert on each family member's credit file.
- Back up the information on your laptop regularly and keep the backup information in a secure location.
- Ensure flash drives are kept secure and files on them encrypted.

QUESTION #33: WHY SHOULD I SAFEGUARD MY FAMILY LUGGAGE WHEN TRAVELING?

Your luggage often tells more of a story about you and your personal life than you realize. As intrusive as it may seem, your luggage contents, such as clothing items, toiletries, personal care items, books, and more, can share what you like and prefer with a thief. Complex items tell an even deeper story about you. Things such as medications in your luggage tell the sifter what ailments you have and what pharmacy you visit. The same is true of your children. Your child's luggage may even go as far as to share his or her school name, emergency contact information, personal hobbies, and schedules of classes or upcoming commitments.

There are two areas of travel concern: family travel and business travel. When vacationing, we tend to travel as a family, where each person has multiple bags and is traveling through an often-confusing process of locations, such as security screening areas, baggage claim areas, airport restaurants, gift shops, or waiting areas. Keeping up with tickets, IDs, luggage, carry-on items, and personal belongings can be challenging.

When traveling for business, we tend to travel alone, but also tend to be more occupied by technology with our computer, BlackBerry, and cell phone usage. Business travelers tend to get caught up in conference calls, business calls, and making future travel arrangements and lose focus on the security of their belongings. The weight of the items we carry sometimes makes it tempting to rest them in an airport chair while we "run" for a quick drink, newspaper, or restroom break. Luggage and personal items left unattended are at a very high risk to be stolen.

Child identity theft occurs every minute of every day. It occurs because we have not yet learned the value of not packing personal information in items that are easily stolen. Identity theft criminals steal luggage, carry-on bags, and computer bags because passengers have a tendency to pack valuable items, sensitive data, and valuable personal information in an unsecure manner. Protecting your child's information begins at home when you make decisions on which items you desire to take with you.

As children age, they are given more and more responsibility to pack bags on their own. School book bags, sports bags, and overnight bags are just a few examples of what children pack every day. Has your child ever returned home to notify you that he or she has left a bag at school, on a sports field, or at a friend's home? What is inside that bag that may put your child's identity at risk? Parents need to be involved in the packing process with their children. Ensure they do not pack identity-sensitive information in their bag or suitcase. Adults should pack only the items necessary for the intended event or travel destination, and refrain from traveling with excess identity documents. Items such as a child's passport should not be taken unless it is necessary for travel out of the country.

During travel, children's personal information should remain with a responsible adult. Identity documents, cash, and sensitive documents must be kept close and accounted for at all times. Checks should be done by parents at intervals to ensure that all items are accounted for. Any suspicious encounters must be reported to parents immediately for evaluation of whether or not it is appropriate to notify law enforcement.

Your bags are always vulnerable throughout your travel journey. From the time you get in a cab or park your car, your personal items become subject to theft. Constant challenges exist, such as the fact that many computer bags, suitcases, and canvas bags look the same. This creates chaos and makes for a good excuse should the thief get caught. All an identity thief has to say is that it looks exactly like their bag or item, and apologize for the "error" for picking up your bag.

Your best defense is to make your item stand out regardless of how common the piece of luggage is. Tie bright-colored ribbon on the handle. Use colored duct tape to mark your bag. Sew a large patch on your bag to set it apart. These are just a few security suggestions that will also allow your child to use his or her creativity to personalize a school or travel bag. Use your imagination to change your bag's appearance.

The hard-core criminals are going to steal no matter what. These are the individuals who are blatant about what they will do and do not care, or those who have employment that provides them special access to your bags when you are not present. Personalizing luggage items discourages criminals who are "on the fence" about stealing.

When traveling, make it a personal policy to always keep your carry-on bag and laptop with you or a family member. The best security for your belongings, and the transportation industry's preference, is to keep them in constant physical contact with you at all times. Establishing a security policy of accountability protects your family from harm.

Your next challenge will be security in your hotel room. When you are outside the room touring and enjoying the sights, both cleaning and maintenance personnel have unlimited access to your belongings. I love to travel, and countless times in the past I have walked hotel hallways seeing open doors where cleaning or maintenance personnel have propped the door open and are multitasking. Lock up both your belongings and your information to protect your family.

QUESTION #34: CAN CHILDREN OF MILITARY PERSONNEL BE TARGETED FOR CHILD IDENTITY THEFT?

One of the most heartbreaking scams I have heard about in quite some time involves the stolen identity of children through the scamming of military spouses. This relatively new scam is generated with a telephone call to a military spouse informing him or her that their deployed spouse has been seriously injured overseas. The caller represents himself or herself as being a representative of the American Red Cross and says that the loved one has been flown to Germany. Treatment in Germany requires notification of the spouse, as well as verbal verification of the serviceman's and family's dates of birth and Social Security numbers. The scammer uses this opportunity to frighten a serviceman's loved one into releasing personal identity information for care to be administered, with no real emergency at hand.

Our U.S. military services are made up of active and reserve forces. Both types of forces are activated for duty assignments around the world in both combat and peaceful duty locations. Our services consist of Army, Navy, Air Force, Marine, and Coast Guard personnel. Military children are like foster children from the single aspect that they move often, encountering multiple caretakers, and attend different school systems where they may spend less time building long-term relationships.

Reserve forces consist of state National Guard units and federal reserve forces. Reserve and National Guard units commonly consist of Air Force Reserve, Army Reserve, Army National Guard, Air National Guard, Coast Guard Reserve, Naval Reserve, and Marine Corps Reserve troops. All services are highly respected and serve proudly. While the commitment of a serviceman is to be held in high regard, the concern related to identity theft is directly associated with a serviceman's need to focus on his or her job.

Military children of reserve and National Guard troops are often left behind in the city, town, or county from which their loved one deployed. Children of active duty troops remain on military posts, bases, or military subsidized housing near the active duty station of the deployed serviceman, as well. Military children lack half of the parenting team to help protect them against child identity theft. Quite honestly, child identity theft is not a parent's major focus when a loved one is deployed, which places a child at greater risk to have his or her personal information stolen.

The best defense military families have is to be among the residents living on an active military installation. Most military installations are closed facilities with full-time police forces. Military police units are quick to respond and thorough in their investigations. They do not usually suffer from the same budgeting woes and department policy problems of local civilian agencies.

Military police organizations are very active in crime prevention. They can assist you with crime prevention information. Contact your military police office or Provost Marshal and inform them you would like a program on identity theft and child identity theft established, if one is not already. If you live off base or post, and you are an active duty family member experiencing child identity theft, you can start with your military police or go to the civilian police agency in the jurisdiction where you live. I would recommend starting with the military police, as this could be a crime targeting you as a military family.

Scams targeting military families are no different than any other specialty scam. Specialty scams target specific situations. Identity thieves evaluate every opportunity to make money and see military situations as unique. Military families need to be aware that vital information, such as an injury or death notification, occur face-to-face and are conducted by military officers in uniform, or credentialed Red Cross personnel. This important notification of a serviceman does not occur by way of telephone or e-mail, so do not release private identifying information.

Service families receiving phone calls requesting any type of personal information need to reject them. Once you receive the call, visit your active duty unit and ask to see the commander in charge. If the unit commander verifies that your incoming call was a scam, ask for a call to be made to the police. A report should be taken so the information can be disseminated to all post or base personnel.

QUESTION #35: IF SOMEONE SENDS MY CHILD A "CHAIN LETTER," IS THERE AN IDENTITY THEFT RISK?

Parents should, at some point, talk to their children about "chain letters." Chain letters are communications circulated by e-mail, over the Internet, through the U.S. postal mail system, or hand delivered child-to-child or adult-to-child. These letters cover a variety of topics, and almost always require the recipient to circulate multiple copies of the letter to friends, relatives, and fellow students.

Chain letters are not limited to children or young adults, but affect savvy adults, as well. Chain letters can be fun, but they can also be destructive. Whether they are fun or destructive, they are designed to be emotionally manipulative to motivate the person who receives them to continue the chain. In most cases, the manipulation behind the desire to circulate chain letters is either fear or superstition. Some letters claim that if you "break the chain," bad luck will come upon you. Other letters say that you may experience death or serious illness if you fail to pass the letter on.

Modern technology has changed the common chain letter. Chain letters are less common as stamped letters you receive in the mail, and more commonly found now as chain texts, chain e-mails, or chain postings on social networking websites. They can reach more children and young adults who are technology savvy. Unfortunately, reaching more children raises concerns of increased exposure to the unknown and additional potential risks to a segment of society that suffers a disproportional amount of identity theft.

Some chain letters involve money and promises of unrealistic or fraudulent success. Chain letters requiring you to send money, and convincing you to enlist others to send money, are illegal. These letters are scams and should be avoided. Chain letters requesting money as an investment in a venture, where you in return will receive hundreds or thousands of dollars, are called "pyramid" schemes. Pyramid schemes often claim that they will be placing your name on a widely circulated list in which the next person to receive the letter will send you money, as will the next person when your name rotates around again, and so on, as a continuous cycle.

The dangers of chain letters are many. They include threats, broken promises, coercive language, and the risk of child identity theft. Letters frequently require children to give their information as part of fulfilling the chain. Whether asked in whole or in part to provide your child's name, address, age, date of birth, and Social Security number, it is all part of the scam.

Chain letters are a way to reach children. Children fail to see the harm in tempting schemes that appear too good to be true. They also see little harm in participating in what seems to be a harmless venture that adds their name and address with hundreds or thousands of others as it circulates around the world. The truth is that when your child receives an e-mail chain letter and chooses to respond, they most likely send the letter to all their contacts.

When this magnifies, hundreds of thousands of children may be impacted and at risk for identity theft.

The impact of chain letters is that your spam will increase threefold, as will your phishing e-mail, worms, viruses, and hoaxes. Once your child's e-mail or phone number is inserted into the circulating list, your computer or phone will be bombarded with virus-infected spam. Your first clue should be a system that is significantly slowed, as well as a notable increase in pop-ups. Your child has now become a target for both sales and scams.

Your best defense is to educate your children on the potential dangers of chain letters and encourage them not to participate. Parents and teachers can partner on this education. Schools can also set policies prohibiting chain letter circulation or participation on school computers. A partnership in education and policies requiring the deleting or shredding of chain letters is your best defense against chain letter dangers.

QUESTION #36: IT IS A NEW SCHOOL YEAR, AND THE FORMS SENT HOME BY THE SCHOOL ASK FOR MY CHILD'S SOCIAL SECURITY NUMBER. AM I REQUIRED TO PROVIDE IT?

Most school systems today are modernized enough to recognize that issuing students identification cards with their Social Security number as their assigned number is unwise. Many of the forms sent home to parents involve emergency notification and insurance. Some forms involve permission to participate in after-school activities. Regardless of the form, the need to provide a child's Social Security number is rare or limited.

My suggestion is to look at each form individually, and if you feel the Social Security number is not needed, discuss the concern of child identity theft with a school administrator. The more forms floating around with your child's Social Security number, the greater chance he or she will become a victim of identity theft. In some cases, forms just need to be updated by the school system removing the request for the Social Security number. In other instances, the request for your child's Social Security number remains on a form because no one has ever challenged it.

You need to inquire about a very important issue when talking to your child's school administration about their Social Security number request on forms. Inquire as to whether the U.S. Department of Education or your state department of education requires the identification of the student on the form you were given. This might actually be the case, depending on the form. If this is the provided explanation, then the school system may be requiring the Social Security number to ensure or verify the number of students for proper funding levels. If there is a federal or state mandate for your child's Social Security number on a form, I suggest you comply.

What if there is no federal or state mandate? If this is the case, three aspects are at work here. The first is old habits. As a society, we have for many, many years identified people not by name but by Social Security number. The second push behind forms sent home requiring a Social Security number could be commercialization. Businesses, such as insurance companies, continue to use Social Security numbers in all their records. Many insurance companies refuse to stop requiring Social Security numbers even though identity theft continues to be a problem. The third aspect is prioritization. Without making the removal of Social Security numbers a priority within our school systems, identity theft will continue to be a threat.

Hard economic times continue to require local school systems to do more with less. School leaders are very concerned with direct security issues, such as the physical safety of their students. Where school systems often fall short in matters of security is in prioritizing all instructional needs over peripheral security concerns, such as child identity theft. To highlight my point, I would challenge you to research how many of our nation's school systems currently have a child identity theft program in place. How about in your own child's school? I bet the answer will surprise you.

The basic question is, do you have to provide your child's Social Security number when it is requested by a school system? Most schools will distribute multiple forms requiring children's Social Security number even if it is not pertinent data. That is your issue. I recommend a visit to your local school administration office to inquire whether they will allow you to omit your child's Social Security number from any form that is not mandated for an acceptable reason. If school administration mandates that the number must be provided, then request an explanation of what security measures are in place to protect your child's Social Security number, and other personal information.

Ask the simple and hard questions. What happens to each form after it is turned in? Who gets it? How is it secured? How long is it kept? Who is responsible for the security of the form? Once the form has been entered into a computer system, what happens to the form and how is the computer information protected? Ask if they shred all documents after their need has passed. While some of this line of questioning may make school administrators uncomfortable due to lack of consistent policies, keep in mind that you are asking these questions to protect the identity of your child.

Protection of your child's personal data is a great area for parents to get involved. Set the tone for the new school year by having the parent-teacher association, parents, teachers, and school administration meet to discuss child identity theft, and the issues surrounding this crime. Parents can make a difference. You can band together and change your school's policies if they do not adequately protect your children. The most memorable changes in society occur with a grassroots movement.

QUESTION #37: MY CHILD REPORTS THAT SOMEONE IS FOLLOWING THEM. COULD IT BE SOMEONE TRYING TO STEAL THEIR IDENTITY?

Child identity theft is a predatory crime. What this means is that someone targets your child to take something from him or her for their own gain. Regardless of the reason, someone following your child is potential danger. In addition to targeting your child for identity theft, your child could be followed for other reasons as well. It could be the surveillance for abduction or a sexual predator scanning the area for potential victims.

In cases of child identity theft, thieves use many different methods of obtaining needed information. One method is when an individual follows children to befriend them to get their information. A strange person will rarely get the information they need, however; a friend will get plenty. To be successful as a thief you must find a method of success.

Befriending by a stranger is concerning, and thieves understand this. Thieves know that contact with a child, if not done in an acceptable or low-key manner, may cause the concern of parents. For this reason, child identity thieves look toward roles in which contact with a stranger is downplayed and they are introduced to children without question. Methods of doing this, for example, can be joining a group that accepts strangers yet includes children, such as a church, volunteering for a scouting troop, or volunteering at a school, library, or museum. They might also look at volunteering or employment with recreational sports leagues.

Befriending also frequently takes place at child-related businesses. From gaming, skating, and teen clothing stores to bowling, biking, and sports businesses, befriending is a door opener. Befriending may also take place at a public place, such as a park, walking trail, recreation area, or at a business. Befriending can take place anywhere and virtually anytime.

Befriending can happen in person or on the Internet. Internet contact can be made through phishing attempts, viruses, chat rooms, teen game rooms, e-mails, and more. People can stalk online just as they can in person. A clue to pick up on is the coincidental occurrence of the same person showing up in person, or online more than once.

Teach your children to report suspicious activity. It is better to err on the side of caution when reporting, so report anything out of the ordinary so a parent or trusted adult can follow up on it immediately. If your child feels he or she is being followed, have your child go to the nearest trusted location and call you. Ensure the trusted location is one that is safe and preferably has an adult who can stay with them until you arrive. Do not assume your child knows to do this. I recognize this sounds simple, and you may have taught your child to seek out an adult if frightened, but in a real-life situation, will he or she react as you taught him or her? Proactive and continuous education in advance of such an encounter is your best preventive measure.

Evaluate the information relayed to you. If you feel it is appropriate, notify the police. Have your child write down all details to include a thorough description of the person of concern, and any vehicle information if appropriate. Get the names of any other children who were present and contact their parents. Ask other children involved to provide any descriptive information they may have to assist law enforcement. If this is a multiple report of similar activity, the police may ask that your child help them develop a sketch composite of the person stalking your child. These steps are critical in assisting law enforcement stop crimes against our children.

Hopefully, your child's report will not be a case of an actual follower. We all know, though, that chances cannot be taken, as clues missed or unreported can lead to devastating consequences. If a stranger has a conversation with your child, the questions asked may help law enforcement determine what type of potential criminal was being sought out. Pedophiles do not usually ask a child for his or her Social Security number. Conversely, child identity thieves generally do not attempt to get your child into a vehicle. Child identity thieves may create small talk, but their desired goal is to get your child's name, birth date, and Social Security number, and move on as quickly as possible to reduce suspicion.

QUESTION #38: MY CHILD PLAYS SPORTS. ARE THERE ANY CHILD IDENTITY THEFT CONCERNS I SHOULD BE AWARE OF?

A large majority of American children play sports. Some play recreational league sports and others play school sports. Some children play on travel teams, while others play for private clubs. Children's sports include baseball, basketball, football, soccer, tennis, and many more. Sports develop children physically, mentally, and socially.

Most leagues, whether recreational, locality affiliated, or school leagues, require a combination of volunteer and paid support. Some recreational league staff members are volunteers who are not paid. These volunteers usually end up being parents or individuals in the local community. Volunteers are a great asset as long as their motives are pure.

School sports are usually governed by a set of state-mandated rules. These rules govern how many practices can be held in a given period of time, how many games can be played in a respective season, and what the standards and rules are for each game. State-developed guidelines establish fair play through mandated rules on specific ages for play in designated grade levels. State leagues also do a good job of following up to ensure compliance.

Recreational leagues set guidelines for play and usually try to mirror collegiate or professional rules. While sports in both recreational and school leagues have rules of eligibility and play, seldom do they spend time developing rules that focus on the security of our children's information. Security of children's information is almost always left to each individual who possesses the data.

Children's sports mirror most of America in that the value of a child's information is not recognized as being critical to protect from theft. Most sports leagues require registration forms and medical physicals. Whether it is a registration form or a physical form, each contains the personal data needed for identity thieves to steal and use a child's information for criminal gain. These same sports leagues, whether recreational or school, do not have large sums of money to purchase high-dollar security programs for their computers or high-security safes to secure their forms.

Most people involved with the administration side of sports will say that the forms are destroyed once they have fulfilled their need. The truth actually is that few can say for sure how long these forms are kept, who is responsible for their destruction, and by what method the forms are destroyed. The method of destruction is critical. Throwing a completed registration or physical form in the trash is the equivalent of posting it on a street sign for anyone to take.

Forms with children's personal information need to be treated with the respect that voting ballots are given if we are to defeat child identity theft. Whether you are involved with a sports league or you are a parent of a child, if you desire to make a difference, commit to getting involved and help change happen. It is as simple as instituting a process and checking to ensure the rules are followed.

Each registration form received should be numbered. Once the data has been entered into a computer, if that is the desired process, it should be destroyed by shredding it with a cross-cutting shredder. A specific person should be designated for this process, and it should be certified by way of a letter that this process has been completed. There should also be a policy against the copying of any registration or physical form once received.

A similar system can be used for medical physicals. Accountability of forms is the best way to protect your child's information. If your league has a system of accountability, it shows that they understand the dangers of child identity theft and care about its participants. If your league is "on the fence" on the issue, they should know that they could be financially liable for a child's information that is lost or stolen by an employee, or volunteer, working within the league's system if there are no policies governing their actions.

QUESTION #39: IF SOMEONE USES MY CHILD'S INFORMATION TO OBTAIN A MORTGAGE, WHAT SHOULD I DO?

Imagine graduating from high school, turning eighteen years old, and being turned down by the college of your dreams because you failed to satisfy the mortgage that was taken out using your name when you were ten years old. How about graduating from college and landing that first and most important job only to be turned down in a background check that reveals you bought a home as an infant and failed to pay what you owed? Welcome to mortgage-related child identity theft.

A quick Internet search on the topic of mortgages and child identity theft will open your eyes to the victims that exist, and the horror stories that haunt them. Most families find out their children have been victimized by debt collection agency notification or issuing of court-related legal proceeding warrants. Most children find out they have been victimized by becoming adults and being turned down for credit or a job. Regardless of how it happens, it still devastates the child and the family.

The first step in resolving mortgage-related child identity theft is to obtain a credit report. As previously mentioned in other areas of this book, obtaining your credit report is free, and it can be done annually. To get the process started, go to the Internet and visit www.annualcreditreport.com. This site will allow you to order your free credit report. When the report is received, view it for fraudulent mortgage activity, and any other fraudulent activity. If you find activity which should not be on your report, it is best to create a child identity theft journal or log book. If you find a mortgage you did not apply for, write the information of the company in your journal or log. You will need to record the business name, address, phone number, amount owed, and account number for further research.

Your next step should be to contact the police. Before doing so, you should consider whether or not your police agency is large enough, and diverse enough, to handle this type of crime. Mortgage fraud involves large sums of money. The FBI has a white collar crimes section that handles mortgage fraud and other types of white collar crimes. Your state police, bureau of criminal investigation, state patrol, or highway patrol most likely have a section that is trained in accounting and mortgage-related crimes. The advantage of working with the FBI is that they have jurisdiction across the United States.

After recording all fraudulent activity in your journal or log, your next contact should be to one of the three major credit reporting agencies to request a ninety-day credit alert. You may contact these at the following addresses:

- Equifax—www.equifax.com
- Experian—www.experian.com
- TransUnion—www.transunion.com

A call to just one of the three major credit agencies will suffice, as the credit bureau who files the alert will notify the two other agencies. The credit alert is good for ninety days, and it is free of charge.

After you contact a credit reporting agency and place your ninety-day alert, make a call to the mortgage company listed on your credit report. Ask to speak to the company's fraud department. Once you have the correct department, advise the representative that your child has been victimized by an identity thief. Give the mortgage fraud representative the name of the law enforcement officer investigating the case as well as the officer's agency name, telephone number, and badge number. This step is important to ensure the mortgage fraud department notates their system in case there is any future activity associated with your name or Social Security number.

Dealing with child identity theft is difficult. When you add serious sums of money to the equation, it becomes even more difficult to resolve. If your child becomes a victim of mortgage-related child identity theft, swift action and police involvement may be the only way to bring resolution to this invasion of your child's identity.

3

DETECTING AND REPORTING IDENTITY THEFT

This critical section of the book will deal with two of the biggest concerns parents have about child identity theft: how to figure out if your child has been victimized and how to report the theft so that the process of cleaning up your child's credit and reclaiming their identity can begin.

QUESTION #40: WHAT ARE SOME EARLY SIGNS THAT MY CHILD IS A VICTIM OF IDENTITY THEFT?

Parents most often overlook the most common sign of identity theft: For no apparent reason, your child begins receiving mail, such as credit card offers. Unless you have opened a bank account recently for your child and the bank is trying to "cross sell" you other financial products, you should not be receiving such mail. Other tip-offs that your child's identity is being used by someone to get credit, or for some other fraudulent purpose, include receiving legal notices, phone calls from debt collectors, and visits from the police.

There are some key points to bring out. Your child's receiving mail does not mean they have been the victim of child identity theft. Even if he or she receives credit card offers, that does not automatically mean they have been victimized. As a parent, you know what actions you have taken on your child's behalf. If you have recently opened up a bank account for your child, the bank may begin to send you information about other account services. Contact your bank and advise them of your preferences for participating in their marketing list, and inquire about their third-party release policy. You have the option to "opt out" of marketing offers, via phone, Internet, mail, or in person, that you do not agree to. If you elect to "opt out," your bank is not allowed to share your information with other parties.

Another reason your child may receive legitimate mail is that you recently obtained an airline frequent flyer card for them. Again, you, as the parent, make the decision about what your child participates in. I would encourage you to "opt out" of anything you are not comfortable with. This does not mean you are "opting out" of a frequent flyer program, for example; just "opting out" of any marketing and third-party lists associated with such a program.

This brings us to the red flags of child identity theft. The most serious indicator that your child has become a victim of identity theft is the receipt of court notices of civil judgment, or court dates for hearings on amounts your child supposedly owes. Legal notices will most likely arrive at your door via a sheriff's deputy or police officer and be hand delivered to you. If you are not present, the law enforcement officer may leave a notice on your door or with someone else at the home, depending on the court's delivery instructions.

Depending upon the circumstances, you might also receive certified legal mail that you are required to sign for. Read the entire letter and contact the court immediately. Take the notice seriously and follow up as soon as possible. Obtain an attorney to represent you if you feel it is necessary.

Watch your U.S. mail for bills received in your child's name from businesses, credit card companies, or debt collectors. Businesses will try to mail bills first when seeking to have debts paid. When payment is not received, creditors resort to collection agencies. Collection agencies seeking to collect on old debts owed will pay to locate the current addresses of people who choose not to pay their obligations. Though a criminal may have used a fake address when obtaining credit in your child's name, a creditor will find you and your child by using legitimate means, such as utility records, property records, and phone number listings. By the time you are located, the bill may be grossly overdue, and collectors will show little sympathy and patience in your plight to clear your name and resolve the outstanding past-due debt.

If an officer shows up at your door asking questions, chances are your family has been victimized. Someone may have used your child's information on a traffic stop or attempted to obtain official documents, such as a driver's license, passport, voter registration card, welfare, or utility services documentation. The individual who stole personal information may have attempted to purchase a gun with the intent to commit a serious crime. My point is that the threat to the victim may range from loss of personal information to serious criminal activity, and much more in between, all of which should be addressed immediately to protect you and your family.

Sit down and discuss what has occurred with the law enforcement officer and cooperate fully, producing all information needed to prove your child's age and identity. There are serious civil ramifications for charging the wrong person with a crime, so the law enforcement officer is going to want to verify all data the police department received, as well as information you provide. In most cases, this information will be provided by law enforcement to the state prosecutor or commonwealth's attorney for guidance on the appropriate course of action.

The Social Security Administration prepares a benefits and earnings statement for those with a Social Security number. This document is used to show annual earnings for Social Security benefits upon an individual reaching his or her eligible retirement age. If anyone has earned income on your child's Social Security number, it will be listed on this statement. If your child has a record of earnings, this is a big red flag unless your child is a young adult and he or she has started working. To obtain a copy of this statement visit www.ssa.gov or call (800) 772-1213.

QUESTION #41: HOW DO ADULT VICTIMS OF CHILD IDENTITY THEFT USUALLY DISCOVER IT?

Finding out that your child has been victimized, or that you were victimized as a child, is like receiving bad news from your doctor. There is never a good way to deliver or receive such devastating news. It is traumatic and long lasting. There are many ways to discover you have been victimized by an identity thief. Discovery can happen as the result of proactive measures, or come to you as a complete surprise.

Most of us would like to think that we would discover our child's victimization as soon as it occurs. Unfortunately, adults who were victimized as children often learn of identity theft the hard way: by being turned down for something they thought was easily obtainable—a first credit card, a student loan, or even a job—all because of bad credit. Your child's victimization might also be discovered during his or her attempt to join the armed services.

Many victims who turn eighteen years old and become adults in the eyes of the legal system find out that they have been victimized when collection agencies contact them. As juveniles, these young adults had no record of services or legal standing in the community. As emancipated adults, they obtain services and driver's licenses, purchase cars, and participate in the employment and financial systems. This participation starts a trail that debt collectors can access and track.

Educating you on how to uncover whether or not your child has fallen victim to identity theft is one of my goals in writing this book. The earlier you can detect your child's victimization, the less damage will occur. Discovering that your child has become a victim means, of course, that the protective measures you put into place were insufficient or nonexistent. I want to arm you with as much information as I know to assist you in child identity theft prevention. Knowledge is power.

No parent desires for their child to be targeted or abused by financial predators. To protect your child, begin by requesting his or her free annual credit report from any of the three major credit reporting agencies. You may contact one of these agencies at the following:

- Equifax—www.equifax.com
- Experian—www.experian.com
- TransUnion—www.transunion.com

If the report you receive advises you that your child does not have a credit record, this is a strong indicator that your child has not been victimized. If this is the case, make a family decision to put into action the preventive measures this book has to offer you.

If you discover that your child does have a credit record, review every detail on the report. This is the point at which you must start your journal or log book. A credit agency report will list businesses, credit card companies, mortgages, and any other entity that issued credit in your child's name. Your first call should be to one of the credit agencies to request that they place a ninety-day fraud alert on your child's account, as I have previously stated. This will prevent the further issuance of credit without your authorization.

Your next call should be to the police to request an investigation into the fraudulent activity. My cautionary note to you is that a certain percentage of child identity theft is perpetrated by relatives. Be prepared for the police to investigate all details and bring forth charges regardless of whether or not there is a relationship to the victim.

You should contact the issuers of accounts in your child's name. Ask to speak with the company's fraud department. Advise the company that your child has been a victim of identity theft and that credit in your child's name should be frozen on the specific account listed in your credit agency report. Ask the fraud representative to confirm, in writing, that your request has been officially notated in their system of record, and confirm any steps to collect delinquent debts. Additionally, contact the credit agency from whom you received your credit report, and request that they notate in their system of record your intent to dispute any amounts owed to any and all creditors.

Discovering child identity theft is not as difficult for parents who are educated on the crime. Knowing your rights helps tremendously. What also helps is the high level of motivation and determination and the bit of anger parents feel; they can channel this into fixing the problem.

QUESTION #42: WHAT IS THE MOST SERIOUS INDICATOR THAT MY CHILD IS A VICTIM OF IDENTITY THEFT?

Devastating news regarding child identity theft may be delivered through many potential avenues. Some include law enforcement notification, certified mail notification, and debt collector contacts. These types of notifications mean that the crime has already been committed against your child, and quick action is needed. The most serious of these is notification brought to you by law enforcement. Though this topic was touched on in question #40, allow me to elaborate on this more in depth.

When a law enforcement officer shows up at your door, you have serious problems that may not be limited to child identity theft. Someone who committed a crime may have used your child's name. If your child is suspected of such an incident, the officer investigating the crime may or may not have obtained a warrant. Many types of crimes are committed with stolen identities. Most usually, these crimes involve some type of fraud.

The most dangerous cases of identity theft are the potentially violent and harmful ones. These crimes may involve cloning your child, or possibly stealing your child's identity to plan, finance, and commit crimes of terrorism. Serious crimes of espionage, or crimes against the United States, require the involvement of federal law enforcement authorities. I would also add that the longer you wait to involve law enforcement, the worse it will be.

If plainclothes officers come to your home or business and present FBI credentials, they may intend to inform you that a terrorist has stolen your child's name. First, ensure that the credentials of the individuals to whom you are speaking are legitimate. Once you determine you are speaking to legitimate law enforcement officers, cooperate fully and completely. Be assured that law enforcement has no desire to charge your child with a crime they did not commit. This does not mean that you would not benefit from having an attorney to provide legal guidance to ensure your family's interests are protected. Listen carefully to what is being conveyed to you, with or without legal representation, cooperate fully, and begin your child identity theft journal or log book.

If your notice does not come in the form of law enforcement delivery, it may come to you as a legal document through certified mail or regular U.S. mail. Certified mail usually indicates one of two things: either a bill is enclosed from a business as a last effort to try to get you to pay it, or it contains a legal notice. In either case, you need to open the envelope and carefully read the letter's contents.

Your initial response will most likely be disbelief and anger, but I encourage you to read the entire communication and key in on critical information. The first critical item to locate in a certified mail delivery is the point of contact for you to contact with questions. Before calling the contact number, start your journal or log book, entering the person's name, business or court name, and phone number. Call the point of contact and schedule a face-to-face meeting.

Resist trying to resolve the issue over the phone unless the business or the court is too far away. If the entity is local, schedule an appointment to discuss your concerns. If need be, and the situation is appropriate, you may desire to take your child with you to the scheduled appointment. If not appropriate, then make sure to bring your child's birth certificate, Social Security card, and a photo along with you. When taking original documentation for verification purposes, try to resolve the issue without giving the business or court the original or a copy.

Whether you hire an attorney for legal advice or not, you need to ensure that there is no negative impact on your child or your child's record. This means that you need to take personal responsibility to ensure your child exits the process without any record of civil judgments, criminal convictions, or negative credit entries. Ask each court, business, or credit agency for written confirmation of this to protect your child in case it comes up again.

QUESTION #43: HOW CAN I FIND OUT FOR SURE IF MY CHILD'S IDENTITY HAS BEEN STOLEN?

Do you know someone who has access to your child's information and had a sudden burst of prosperity? Have you been denied government benefits or assistance because you were told that your child is already receiving assistance? Has your child's passport application been denied because he or she already has one on file? Are you receiving calls from bill collectors or businesses looking for your child?

If you experience any one of these signs, or other signs mentioned in this book, you need to start the process of verifying that your child's financial future is still intact. If warning signs are present, quick action is imperative, as your child may be a part of the national statistic that indicates that children are fifty-one times more likely than adults to succumb to identity theft. Finding out one way or another will give you the peace of mind needed to sleep at night.

If you believe that your child's identity has been tampered with, you owe it to yourself, and your child, to verify if it is true. Unfortunately, unlike most crimes, child identity theft cannot be verified by a trip to your local or state police office. Law enforcement agencies do not maintain databases that can determine whether a child or an adult has been victimized until it is reported as a crime.

This being the case, the first thing you will need to do to find out if your child's identity has been stolen is obtain his or her credit report. This can be done by contacting one of the three major credit reporting agencies. You may contact them at the following:

- Equifax—www.equifax.com
- Experian—www.experian.com
- TransUnion—www.transunion.com

Of the three agencies, TransUnion is currently the only agency to offer a secure online form process when ordering a credit report for a child. Both Experian and Equifax require the parent or legal guardian to print a credit report request form that must be mailed into the agency upon completion.

If there is not a report for your child, that's a pretty good indicator that no one has attempted to get credit in your child's name. This is welcome news, but you should not let your guard down. The reality is you need to get updated, educated, and working on protective measures to ensure the safety of your child's identity. If your child does have a credit report, then there is a good chance that she or he has been victimized. If your child has in fact been victimized, start your child identity theft journal, record the entry from the credit report you are concerned about, contact one of the three credit reporting agencies, and place your free ninety-day credit alert; then call the police. By now, I hope some of this advice is starting to sound repetitive, and familiar. Your action now is louder than my words.

Another helpful document is a Social Security Administration benefits and earnings statement. These statements can be ordered from the U.S. Social Security Administration's website at www.ssa.gov/mystatement/. Review for income your child did not earn, and notify the Social Security Administration of any error. Take the information you learn from the benefits statement and file a police report on any child identity theft crime.

These are the two "for-sure" mechanisms to verify child identity theft. Other signs mentioned throughout this book give cause for concern, but the credit report and Social Security Administration's benefits and earnings statement provide you with proof. The good news is that neither of these requires a fee, and both are simple to obtain.

Now it is time to remove your children as a potential statistic. Verification is just one of several steps, but an important one. If you have discovered that your child has not been victimized, then help others learn about the crime of identity theft. If your child has been victimized, then use the information you have read in this book to regain control of your child's financial future.

Use your verification findings as your peace of mind; however, do not allow a one-time check lead you to believe that your family cannot be victimized in the future. Annual credit checks are necessary until your child becomes an adult and can request his or her own credit report. Your child may not thank you right now, but he or she will certainly appreciate your efforts in the future.

QUESTION #44: WHAT SHOULD I DO IF MY CHILD STARTS TO RECEIVE BILLS IN THE MAIL?

Since I was a child, one of my favorite things to do has always been going to the mailbox to retrieve the mail. I did this knowing that only one in one hundred letters would be for me. In looking back, I believe it was the joy of seeing my name on the envelope, and the hope that there was something good on the inside, that kept me intrigued with mail delivery. Strangely enough, even today, I like going to the mailbox in the hope of finding a nice note or card, although most of what I receive now are household bills.

Retrieving mail from the mailbox is seemingly an elementary task, and easily one that a child could handle. The dangers that exist today in society mandate that while children can retrieve the mail, an adult should screen it before opening. This is due to the uniqueness of the crime of child identity theft and child predators. Screening allows parents to see who is sending their children mail. Just for a moment, imagine what an impact parents could have if we had the same control over e-mail.

The fact alone that a child is receiving mail does not itself indicate that he or she has been victimized. Critical factors about mailings to children and identity theft should raise your awareness or suspicion. The first factor is mail volume. Is your child receiving an unusual amount of mail? The second factor is who is sending the mail and how they send it. As you have already learned from information covered in this book, preapproved credit card offers, bills, mortgage offers, car loan offers, lottery mail, and other mail that seems out of the ordinary for a child to receive, may be red flag warnings of child identity theft.

Children do not usually receive bills in the mail unless you have ordered something in their name or allowed them to order something that requires a billed payment. When dealing with child identity theft, it is not unusual for children whose identities have been compromised to receive bills in the mail from retailers, credit card companies, debt collectors, banks, mortgage lenders, electronics stores, or auto dealers.

In most cases of identity theft, the criminal will use your child's name, date of birth, and Social Security number, but change his or her address to avoid detection. Businesses seeking to collect on debts owed will pay for debt collectors to find your child's name. These debt collectors use computer systems targeting public records to locate current addresses of people who choose not to pay their obligations. They will relentlessly call homes with your last name asking if your child is there or if the person receiving the call knows your child.

Collection agencies will also use legitimate means, such as tax records, utility records, court documents, property records, and other public records, to locate any individual delinquent on a debt. By the time the collection agencies use all these resources, the bill will be grossly overdue. Debt collectors will eventually find your child and start calling, wanting you to pay the debt whether you were victimized or not. Collectors will also start a campaign of harassing mail and contact you at your place of employment in an attempt to get you to pay the bill.

Your success is found in your ability to communicate your predicament. Look for that point of contact in communications your child receives. Contact the appropriate point of contact and arrange a time to meet or, if they are too far away, explain that your child has been victimized by identity theft. In addition to the collectors, call the business or creditor who is reporting the debt directly and advise them of the same. Businesses want to collect on past-due debts but do not want to get sued in the process.

If you feel legal representation is needed, obtain an attorney and have him or her write to each company or organization reporting erroneous information to advise them that your child has fallen victim to identity theft and that your child does not owe any respective debt they are reporting. Mentioning that further contact would be considered harassment might help. Lastly, remember to keep your journal or log book of phone calls, letters, contacts, and any information that was discussed, then contact the police to report your child's victimization. Recalling information through your journal or log book will help tremendously when you are talking to creditors, as they will know that you are serious about the identity theft and not just trying to skip out on a legitimate bill owed.

QUESTION #45: WHAT ACTIONS SHOULD I TAKE BEFORE I MAKE THE CALL TO THE POLICE?

Be realistic about what you are about to take part in. I believe the average child identity theft victim and the child's parent(s) and/or guardian(s) will spend approximately 500 hours, and between $3,000 to $5,000 of their own money, in their attempt to report and correct identity theft victimization. Documenting, reporting, writing letters, making phone calls, and investigating identity theft cases are an exhausting process for parents and guardians. The actions you take prior to beginning the cleanup stage can mitigate some of the negative aspects and soften the blow of this long and painful process.

The first step is mental preparation. The better you mentally prepare yourself before you begin the process, the better you will deal with what you are about to face. Understand the time and commitment required in dealing with child identity theft. The process will entail making a lot of phone calls, writing in journals, writing letters, talking to police officers, going to court, talking to creditors, visiting businesses, and more.

Amid all the devastation of having your child's financial future stolen will be the creditors and debt collectors. Debt collectors have one goal, and that is to collect money due to them. They are not concerned with your issues, challenges, or problems, which in this case revolve around child identity theft. Expect debt collectors to be pushy and unsympathetic. Success in dealing with them involves your pushing back by telling them that your child has been harmed because they continue to harass you with false information. Tell the debt collectors that you are contemplating legal action against them if the harassment does not stop.

If your child is a victim of identity theft, the first step in cleaning up the mess is going to be developing a journal of events. Regardless of the agency contacted, one of the key points of success will be "note making." A journal, which can be as simple as a legal pad or composition notebook, provides you a permanent record of actions. The journal needs to list the date of each call or contact, agency contacted, person spoken with, e-mail address or return phone number, a description of what was said, and a list of what actions need to be taken as a result of the contact.

In addition to a journal, I recommend that you maintain an accordion-type folder to store letters, bills, receipts, notes, business cards, document copies, and other information you will need to retain. The better organized you are, the easier it will be to quickly reference a needed item. I also recommend that you never give away an original document unless required to by the court. Make extra copies for creditors or organizations who are in need of proof or documentation of a matter at hand, but retain the most legible document, preferably the original.

Once you have the journal in place, gather documents and records you need to have on hand before you call the police. Before you make the call to law enforcement, I highly recommend you gather any bills, mail, insurance statements, credit agency reports, credit card statements, birth certificates, and any other pertinent information you have available to you as proof to support your claim. Having these documents readily available will assist you in answering the questions that will be asked of you by the law enforcement officer or representative who takes your call. If you do not have copies of critical documentation to best explain your situation over the telephone, it may be easier to visit the police department in your local area for a face-to-face meeting. If you do not have copies of your original documentation, local law enforcement can assist you with this, as well, when you report the crime.

Whom you call depends on where you live and the agencies available to service you. If you live within city or town jurisdictions, you will most likely want to contact your local city or town police department. If you reside outside city or town limits, your options will be the state police or your local county or parish sheriff's office. If you are unsure of whom to call, contact your state police, state patrol, or state bureau of criminal investigation department and ask them to whom the crime should be reported.

QUESTION #46: HOW AND WHEN SHOULD I REPORT CHILD IDENTITY THEFT TO THE POLICE?

Child identity theft is like a cancer. If you do not put an end to child identity theft, it will grow to a point that will overwhelm you and your family, so let's get started. Businesses or legal entities, such as a court, will not believe you have really been victimized if you have not contacted the police. Also, some banks, creditors, credit agencies, insurance companies, loan institutions, and business organizations have policies that preclude working with you unless you have a police report.

A big problem law enforcement agencies across the nation are experiencing is a lack of reporting by child identity theft victims. This fact is exposed in great detail in the Federal Trade Commission's Identity Theft Survey Report.[1] This report states that 74 percent of all identity theft victims, regardless of age, do not contact the police. Unreported child identity theft makes it impossible to accurately quantify the number of actual victims.

Once you make the decision to call the police and have prepared the items you need, call them. Options will be available for reporting your crime. You can call and request to have a law enforcement officer meet you, or you can go to the police station or sheriff's office and have an officer take a report. While either is acceptable, you have taken the first and most important step in starting the process, which is to report child identity theft.

If a patrol officer, deputy, or trooper takes your initial report, ask if he or she intends to work the case personally, or if your case will be reassigned to a detective, investigator, or special agent. You are probably asking yourself now why this information matters. Well, it does. Any of the officers within the respective agency could work the crime, and most would do a good job given the factors I am about to discuss. Your goal, however, should be to ensure a law enforcement official with experience and knowledge of child identity theft, with time to work your case, is assigned to you. It does not matter what department they work for, or whether they are dressed in uniform or dress clothes, what matters is that the officer assigned to your case has the knowledge and availability to focus on your child and his or her stolen identity.

Your priority between the two should be knowledge of the crime. If the officer has not been trained on the aspects and intricacies of child identity theft, and the laws of identity theft, then he or she may have the available time to work on the case, but there may be a lot of wasted time due to lack of knowledge. Availability of the officer is the other issue, and this is dictated by work caseload. If you are assigned an investigator, detective, or special agent who is overworked with a high caseload, then your case will probably sit with limited attention. You do not want this either. Be proactive and ask questions of the law enforcement officer taking the initial report with the goal of getting your child's case into the hands of the most knowledgeable and available investigator.

Be prepared for the possibility that the person taking the initial report may not be the one assigned to investigate your case. This is normal and the accepted procedure in many law enforcement agencies across the country. If the law enforcement officer you speak with initially tells you that the report will be forwarded to a detective bureau, investigations section, or bureau of criminal investigation, ask he or she when you can expect to receive a phone call. Also ask the officer for a name and contact phone number of the appropriate person in case you do not receive the phone call in a reasonable period of time.

You may not be able to obtain a copy of the initial police report for a few days after reporting the crime, so ask the officer you speak with in the initial conversation for a case number. In most cases, the officer can contact their dispatch area to have a case number assigned before the initial meeting concludes. Ask the officer when you can expect to receive a hard copy police report, the procedure for obtaining one, and if there are any costs associated with getting a copy of the report. When you finish meeting with the law enforcement officer, regardless of the location, double-check your paperwork to ensure you still have all of your original documents.

Now that you have filed a report with law enforcement, it would be a good time to sit down and check items off your list that you should have accomplished at this point:

- Obtained a credit report
- Requested a Social Security benefits and earnings statement
- Created a journal
- Contacted a credit reporting agency requesting a ninety-day fraud alert
- Purchased an accordion-type file storage folder for letters and documents
- Highlighted all documents for points of contact, amounts owed, and any court dates
- Saved copies of any suspicious mail or e-mails

QUESTION #47: WHAT SHOULD I KNOW ABOUT WORKING WITH THE POLICE ON A CHILD IDENTITY THEFT CASE?

The best advice I can give you in reference to dealing with the police is to try not to be "annoying" but BE PERSISTENT in all phases of your police investigation. Few police agencies have an identity theft unit, and even fewer totally understand the crime of child identity theft and the wide range of methods used. They know this type of crime involves fraud, but may steer away from it if at all possible due to a lack of specialized personnel, lack of manpower, and most importantly, solvability reasons.

The same applies to police officers. Most police officers view child identity theft as a new crime buzzword that they somewhat understand but for which they have little or no training to investigate. If law enforcement does not understand child identity theft, they will be hesitant to fully investigate the case. Whether meeting with the initial law enforcement officer, or any individual subsequently assigned to your case, make sure to ask if he or she will be the investigating officer, and if they have received training on investigating child identity theft.

Fortunately for most police officers, the majority of child identity theft crimes have hard facts that can be traced, thoroughly investigated, and solved. An international criminal certainly could steal your child's identity through the use of computer phishing, text, spam e-mails, spoofing, or phone conversations, but it is equally to more likely that it will happen from within the United States.

While most child identity theft is more likely to happen in the United States, a significant amount of fraud is committed against adults and businesses from outside the United States. Most of these cases are Nigerian scams. Nigerian scams come in many different varieties, but the basic premise is that they are able to con you out of money with a scheme they make you believe is true. An example of this is an unknown individual calls or e-mails you to notify you that he or she is contacting you on behalf of a friend or family member who is in distress. The caller or individual who sent the e-mail insists that money is needed immediately via wire transfer to remedy the situation. Under no circumstances should you ever wire funds, or release personal information, to an unknown source. Other Nigerian scams include mail fraud investment schemes and lottery-winning scams. Nigeria is just one of the foreign countries from which theft scams are on the rise, though it is not the only one. I mention this because credit card companies get burned so often, they have developed policies to forgive debts, both national and international, incurred by cardholders as the result of fraud. Credit card companies forgive fraud debt so frequently that police officers are not energized to investigate what credit card companies are not willing to prosecute.

The last issue you face is jurisdictional challenges and the ability to investigate. Local police officers are challenged when it comes to investigating crimes committed by thieves outside of their jurisdiction. Law enforcement officials may gather facts and evidence from the victim, obtain a subpoena for online provider information, and interview local suspects, but jurisdictional limitations are a consideration of how your case will be assigned and investigated. Lack of proper budgeting and funding may hamper their efforts to travel great distances to investigate details of your case.

Officers with state authority can travel across the state, but face similar challenges when investigating details in other states. Federal authorities have jurisdiction across the United States, to include local law enforcement agencies. When the crime is international, there is little chance anything can be done. Federal authorities can work with Interpol on large issues, but it is doubtful that individual crimes will be investigated.

Remember when speaking with a law enforcement officer that quite often child identity theft is committed by criminals who have had physical contact with your child. This contact may have been at a business, school, or location that your child frequents, or more concerning, to your home. These factors make child identity theft solvable. Use this to your advantage when speaking with the officer. Credit card companies electing not to prosecute criminals will neither undo the harm caused to your child nor prevent it from happening to another child. You must be persistent.

Organizing your facts and documents will impress the investigating officer. Organization sets a positive tone for making the officer believe you can help them solve the case because you are detailed in your record keeping. Law enforcement always prefers a solved case versus an unsolved, open matter related to a child; the assigned officer is also allowed personal satisfaction in a closed case. Help them understand that your case can be brought to a logical conclusion with a conviction with your cooperation.

QUESTION #48: WHEN SHOULD I CONTACT THE POSTAL SERVICE INSPECTOR REGARDING A STOLEN IDENTITY?

The U.S. Postal Inspection Service is the law enforcement branch of the federal government that deals with U.S. mail. They are charged with investigating any crime that involves our mail. The U.S. Postal Inspection Service is one of the best advocates you can find when your crime involves child identity theft, or identity theft.

Postal inspectors can assist you, for example, if a criminal steals your child's identity and subsequently submits a change of address, allowing newly obtained credit cards to go to the criminal's address of choice and not yours. They can investigate suspicious mail your child is receiving. They can investigate any case where your residential mail is stolen. Postal inspectors have jurisdiction across the United States and generally do a thorough job of following through with investigations.

In addition to investigating identity theft connected to the mail, postal inspectors should be credited with the best proactive fraud services available among the federal agencies. The U.S. postal service inspectors have produced several identity theft videos, such as:[2]

- *Identity Crisis*—the story of identity theft
- *Truth or Consequences*—check scams
- *All the King's Men*—recovering from financial crime
- *Web of Deceit*—the prevention of Internet fraud
- *Long Shot*—foreign lottery scams
- *Dialing for Dollars*—telemarketing investment fraud
- *Nowhere to Run*—international efforts to stop fraud
- *Work-at-Home Scams: They Just Don't Pay*—scams involving work-at-home offers

To view these videos, visit the U.S. Postal Inspection Service website at www.postalinspectors.uspis.gov.

I also encourage you to view the Consumer Awareness section on the same website.[3] This section maintains great public information on the following topics:

- ID theft
- Reshipping scams
- Money order scams
- Internet scams
- Work-at-home scams
- Dialing for dollars
- Sweepstakes
- Victim rights

Visit the U.S. Postal Inspection Service website mentioned above. If you require any service outlined, their website is user friendly: victims can fill out online forms and submit them directly from the website. The following crimes are reportable on the website: mail theft, mailbox vandalism, identity theft, mail fraud, and false change of address. The website also offers victim assistance information.

You may also view the U.S. Postal Inspection site to educate yourself on the latest scams that involve the mail, or to look at the latest wanted posters. You can check out press releases on crimes solved. Use this site to obtain a complaint form if you are the victim of a mail-related crime. Lastly, check out the same Internet site to find your nearest U.S. postal inspector, or visit your local post office for help.

QUESTION #49: WHAT INFORMATION DO I NEED TO PROVIDE AS EVIDENCE OF IDENTITY THEFT?

Most jurisdictions have an advocate within the prosecutor's office called a victim witness coordinator, or victim assistant, waiting to help a victim with their identity theft crime. You may feel that you are on your own when it comes to gathering information and documentation and proving your case, but you are not. You need to reach out for help. Whether you choose to contact someone for help or not, let's discuss what you will need to succeed in proving your case.

The first question I would pose is, how did you first find out about the crime? Was it a piece of mail that raised your suspicion? Was it a bill collector that called you? Did you get a U.S. Social Security Administration benefits statement with erroneous information on it? Was it information from your insurance carrier on a medical procedure your child did not have?

Proving child identity theft means building your case through documentation that something criminal occurred. Start with the documents you have, such as your child's birth certificate. Second, locate a recent photo of your child, so you can show the picture along with your supporting documentation, as you try to convince accusing people, companies, and agencies that your child is not the person out there applying for credit. Third, have your child present when you speak with the police, if appropriate. This may seem like a frightening consideration, but it is an important step in building your case.

If anyone can act as your advocate to advise creditors that your child is in fact not the person the creditor believes he or she is, it will be the police officer investigating the case.

I previously mentioned the need to purchase an accordion-type folder. Organize this folder into sections for the following: bills received, letters written, credit agency reports and correspondence, police report copies, court documents, and attorney correspondence. Include a section for your child's personal information, such as the birth certificate and photo. Find a system that you are comfortable with, such as using a yellow sticky note to designate your original document, so you never give it away. These suggestions may sound logical, but the process may become overwhelming if you do not keep very good records in an organized manner.

Investigators want to know why it is you think your child has become a child identity theft victim. Why did someone steal your child's name, date of birth, or Social Security information? If your discovery began with a letter from the Internal Revenue Service, this is what you want to show the officer. The same applies to a court notice. Help the officer by showing them your journal of creditors, businesses, or organizations you have called, written to, or visited in your attempt to clear up the fraudulent activity against your child.

If you speak with a business, ask the associates or employees what the person who bought their product(s) looked like. Make sure to write down their description and provide that information to the investigator. Make sure to ask what time of day the purchase occurred, as well as all serial numbers of the items purchased, if applicable, in case the police are able to obtain a search warrant at a later date. Try to get copies of bills of sale from any business, as well as copies of any documentation the fraudster signed. Last, if the store where items were bought had video surveillance, ask the manager to preserve it for the police, and then immediately advise the investigator assigned to your case.

What have been covered thus far are thefts of a smaller scale. Imagine uncovering information that reveals your child's name has been used to purchase an expensive investment, such as a vehicle or home. If this is the case, you will want to visit the bank, lender, or auto dealer and ask them for copies of any documents related to the purchase. Prepare yourself mentally; they will probably not want to provide the documents to you. What is important to note here is that the company from whom you are requesting the documents believes that the criminal is in fact the "real" individual with your child's name. Their resistance to release documentation is acceptable, as the company may be worried about being sued by either you or the person to whom they sold the item.

Convey to agencies or companies you are approaching that you are trying to clear up a case of child identity theft and that you are a parent. Do the same with anyone not willing to give you documentation. If an agency or company is not willing to comply with your request for documentation, provide this information to the police. Law enforcement can obtain a subpoena for the information, and force the business or organization to comply. If this does not work, you can hire a private attorney and ask him or her to petition the court for the documents. This part of the process may be very emotional and frustrating. Do not allow the situation to escalate by demanding documentation in such a way that you become part of the problem, and not the solution. Reach out for legal or law enforcement help to assist you with this process.

QUESTION #50: AS A PARENT, IF I AM A VICTIM OF IDENTITY THEFT, DOES IT RAISE THE CHANCES THAT MY CHILD MIGHT BE, AS WELL?

Most adults experiencing an identity theft crisis never think to check their children's credit file for abuse. The majority of victims never even check their spouse's file. Identity theft is personal, emotional, and devastating and quite frequently causes a "tunnel vision"-type effect. Stealing one's name, birth date, or Social Security number violates the victim, causing trauma that creates insecurity and confusion.

Victims often feel lost and unsure of whom to go to. If you call your local police, they may or may not be experienced in investigating identity theft, while a federal police agency might say the dollar amount of the loss is too low for them to get involved. Dealing with these types of issues can cause a victim to lose focus on the fact that they might not be the only victim.

Another contributing factor can be the lack of knowledge of exactly who stole your identity and how they committed the crime successfully. Not knowing this can give you the false sense of security that you were a random victim. The truth might be that the thief was someone who cleans your home, services your home, or burglarized your home, without stealing anything; or, it could quite possibly be a relative.

Knowing how the theft was committed can be vital information because it can subtract the "random" effect and give immediate rise to the suspicion that other family members could be at risk. You can help yourself by reviewing the credit report you request very carefully to determine if there is any connection between the business where an account was opened, and the people with whom you associate.

It is also important to look for a clue in what was purchased. If, for example, you discover a credit card was obtained in your name and the criminal used the card to purchase furniture, you should be asking yourself if you are aware of any relative or friend who may have recently purchased new furniture. If an account was opened in your name, does your credit report show what address the thief used? In cases such as child identity theft, the thief will believe that you will never find out about the theft, or convince himself or herself that they will be long gone by the time you do, so they might list their actual address.

If you review your credit report and it says that a purchase was made in which a delivery was required, ask the reporting company to provide you with the address to which the delivery was made. If a purchase was made in your name, you have the right to know what address the item was shipped to. Ask the business to provide you with a copy of all records of purchase, payment, and delivery. Look for telephone numbers used. Do you recognize the telephone number used as a contact? Is it a friend, relative, or service provider that has access to your home? Ask the delivery drivers if they are able to provide a description of the individual(s) to whom the items were delivered. Each piece of information uncovered will help law enforcement move forward with your case.

All of the questions mentioned above are important because they indicate that your family can be at greater risk for identity theft since you were victimized. While the fact that you have been victimized alone does not mean your family may have been, as well, it may mean that they might be next. The identity thief may have started his or her criminal intentions with you, but may have a plan to move to your spouse and children as his or her next victim. Keep in mind the criminal already has your home or other identifying address.

To protect your family, take the following steps if you are victimized. First, request a credit report for all members in your household. Second, place a free ninety-day credit alert on the credit file of all family members by calling any one of the credit-issuing agencies. Next, report the victimization to the state, county, or local police. This protects you and your family from debt collectors and creditors. Last, but not least, go to the website for the Federal Trade Commission, www.ftc.gov, and file an identity theft complaint. Remember to obtain a copy of your complaint report for your records, and record all actions taken in your journal or log book.

QUESTION #51: WHY ARE MILITARY PARENTS OFTEN TARGETED FOR IDENTITY THEFT?

In the late 1960s, the Department of Defense switched from using service numbers to identify military service personnel to using their Social Security

Administration–assigned Social Security numbers for all tracking. This trend continued until 2009, when the Pentagon phased out the use of all but the last four digits of the number. According to the *Army Times*,[4] this new 2009 four-digit system, used along with other identifying personal data, was accepted as "common practice in the private sector."

Service personnel, whether active duty, reserve, or National Guard, were identified for more than fifty years by their Social Security numbers for pay, medical services, insurance, identification, equipment issuance, and more. Having spent twenty-five years in the military reserves, I can tell you firsthand that your Social Security number was what you were identified by. From the medical and dental charts that documented every shot given and cavity filled, to the infamous Leave and Earnings Statement that was issued at each pay period, your Social Security number defined you.

Identity thieves have always targeted service personnel. They share a similar characteristic with those who experience modern-day child identity theft. This characteristic is an extremely long period in which they are, or could be, disconnected from financial credit services, creating a prolonged period by which identity theft can be discovered. For military members, I am talking about overseas deployments. Whether these deployments were long tours away from home in a foreign country, or fighting in a combat zone, the deployment period left the servicemen disconnected from what could be occurring with their identity.

A famous symbol of military members is the iconic green canvas "duffle" bag. Regardless of the service, Army, Air Force, Coast Guard, Marine Corps, or Navy, personnel were required to put their Social Security number on their bag. This number was accompanied by their name and rank. What a gift to a modern-day identity thief.

Identity thieves could visit airline terminals, noting information on the bags as they moved throughout the airport. These bags contained the two critical pieces of information: name and Social Security number. The serviceman's address, for an identity thief, was neither wanted nor needed, as they planned to divert credit card applications, loan applications, vehicle purchases, and business revolving account billing to their own address, or a fake address created for illegal purposes.

Most identity thieves work very little for their income. In the case of military members, thieves visit secondhand military surplus stores that make their living selling used military personal equipment items, such as duffle bags. The criminals also sell any other type of personal equipment, such as old uniforms, helmets, belts, and other items, that also identified a serviceman's name, rank, and Social Security number.

If a serviceman bought an item they planned to use for work, they would still put their Social Security number, name, and rank on it. This identified it as theirs, as it was an accepted common practice through all services. Items without identification would quite often become the property of a general holding area, never to be reclaimed by its rightful owner.

This same type of system followed service personnel into retirement. Airmen, soldiers, sailors, Marines, and Coast Guardsmen who left military service and sought follow-up medical care with the Veterans Administration were identified by their name, address, and Social Security number. The frequency of identity theft has forced the government as a whole to change.

QUESTION #52: WHY IS CHILD IDENTITY THEFT A PROBLEM FOR MILITARY CHILDREN?

Military children face two distinct challenges in reference to child identity theft. The first is the fact that military families move so often. The second is the deployment of one or both parents for long periods of time. These two issues create insecurity and make these children vulnerable to child identity thieves.

Military children of active-duty personnel have for many, many years been affectionately referred to as "military brats." Their cultural identity involves high mobility and seldom settling down for more than a year or two. While children get used to the frequent moving or long periods without a parent, they never enjoy the lack of stability.

Each and every military family finds themselves in the same situation. Military children become resilient and seem to find comfort in knowing other children around the world wherever they are stationed. This is quite possibly a small consolation, as frequent moves make them similar to foster children in one aspect: moving often.

In a military child's educational lifetime, he or she may attend a new school each year. Moving often sends a child's personal information out to more people, thus increasing your chances of theft. Each school attended maintains files and a database with each student's personal information. While a file or transcript may be sent to a new school, student data is seldom completely deleted.

Not only do current teachers have access to your child's date of birth and Social Security number, but so do office staff, principals, and higher headquarters personnel, such as the local board of education. If you have a child who attended six different schools, for example, you would probably be amazed to find out that all six schools still maintain information on your child. The school system in which your child attended his or her school may be required to maintain past student information for audit purposes, or simply be negligent in not deleting it.

A common misconception is that all military children go to military schools on active posts. While this was the norm years ago, it is not today. It is much more cost effective for the Department of Defense to pay a fee to the local school district for children of military servicemen to attend its schools than to hire educators, faculty, and maintenance employees to maintain schools on post. In most cases, military children attend public schools in the communities surrounding the military installation.

In a military family, quite often one or both military parents are deployed. With identity theft at an all-time national high for children, military dependents need constant protection. The volatility of military life focuses attention in other areas, such as constant worry about the safe return of a loved one. Identity theft may have priority in civilian life, but again, as with foster children, many other issues of concern distract a military family from implementing a proper child identity theft plan.

So what are military families to do? With frequent moves, families need to make checklists to ensure they do not forget anything with each relocation. In and among the checklist items should be child identity theft issues. Visit the school and meet with a school counselor, faculty member, or the principal to discuss your child's records. Ask what documentation will be sent or hand carried to the new school and, more importantly, what will be left behind.

Use this same mindset in dealing with any other connection your child may have with community entities. From doctor and dentist offices, to community libraries and sports leagues, find out what each has on file as documentation regarding your child, and why any information needs to remain in their records if you leave the area.

You can also help other military families by finding the military community service entity on your post or base. Assist in developing checklists and policies that address child identity theft. You may find that you have to carry the torch and spread the word as identity theft thrives, but child identity theft lurks behind the scenes. Make it a priority issue for your installation.

QUESTION #53: MY CHILD HAS RECEIVED A TOY CATALOG IN THE MAIL IN THEIR NAME. IS THIS A SIGN THAT THEY HAVE BEEN TARGETED FOR IDENTITY THEFT?

If your child receives a catalog in the mail from a toy store, you might ask yourself if he or she has been targeted for identity theft. This may, or may not, be the case. It is important to know your child's mail-receiving patterns, store memberships, and web-surfing patterns and habits. This information will help you determine what is normal, what is unusual, and what you need to investigate.

For a parent to worry about any aspect of their children's lives is understandable. The good news is that parents and guardians are in the best position to know the signs of change in a child's life. You can set family policies and double-check systems to help protect your children. One of your best protections will be mail policies.

A good protective family policy addresses the proper way to check the mailbox for mail. If you currently allow your children to check the daily mail in the mailbox, do you have them bring it to you first for examination? Examining the mail gives you the opportunity to see who is sending information in your child's name. This also provides you with an opportunity to review what individual or company is sending mail to your child, from what address the mail is being sent, and any identifying postmark on the letters or packages. One clue to look for in mail is bulk versus first class. If the mail you received is bulk mail, it most likely has been sent to more than just your child. This is the case with sale papers, circulars, and business mail.

Personal mail is usually sent first class and specifically to your child. First-class mail is usually sent by businesses or individuals, and may often appear with handwritten information versus businesses that type or generate mailings by computer. Both can be concerning, but handwritten is more personal and may deserve more of your attention. In addition to identity theft, you could uncover a predator your child has met online who is now sending your child mail.

If you allow your children to get the mail in your absence, instruct them not to open or tamper with any envelope or package that arrives at your home in his or her name until you can review it. While this may sound overprotective, it is intended to be. Children are creatures of habit, and if taught how to properly handle incoming mail correspondence at an early age, the proper plan will be in place to protect all members of your household from identity theft. If this step saves your child from becoming the victim of a crime, it is worth it. If you find a mailed item of concern, contact local law enforcement and secure the information for investigation.

Catalogs you receive in the mail are just attempts to lure you into a store or to a website to purchase items, goods, or services. If your child receives a toy catalog and it is the only one they have received this month, you probably have little to worry about. If your child has registered at the store, or on their website as a customer, then you are probably fine, as well. If your child went to the store's Facebook page and "liked" or "friended" the store, then it is unlikely your child has been victimized.

What if you have done none of these steps, though? Could your child have been targeted for child identity theft? The answer is yes. In most cases, children involve themselves with computer-related scams through free offers, prize registrations, and game-related offers. The "spin-off" of registering may be magazine offers, unwanted subscriptions to services, and the theft of their identity.

It is rare that a website or e-mail offer gives something for free without requiring an individual to enter his or her name, address, and probably their phone number. Some offers even ask for date of birth and/or Social Security number. Most websites or e-mails will claim that the reason for requiring personal information is to verify age. Regardless of whether or not the offer is legitimate, the potential for danger exists.

Your best defense is to contact a business that sends your child mail and ask them how they obtained your child's information. If the company received your child's information because your child registered himself or herself, then you need to have a conversation with your child about the dangers of releasing identifying information to unknown individuals. If you have concerns, you can always contact your local postal inspector. Regardless of whether your child did or did not give the person or business his or her personal identifying information, I encourage you to advise the person you speak with to remove your child from all mailing lists and future offers. Mailings and "free" offers should be limited to the ones parents preapprove, and no more.

4

DEALING WITH CHILD IDENTITY THEFT

This section will provide nuts-and-bolts advice on how to clean up the damage done to your child's credit if he or she becomes a victim of identity theft.

QUESTION #54: WHAT ARE THE DIFFERENT TYPES OF CHILD IDENTITY THEFT VICTIMS?

There are two main types of victims; the first is a child whose parents discover he or she has been victimized while still a child. I call this individual a "child" victim, since knowledge is obtained while the child is still young. The second type of victim is one who discovers, once he or she becomes an adult, that they were victimized as a juvenile. I will refer to these individuals as "adult/juvenile" victims.

As one could imagine, there are no advantages to either status. Children victimized by adult financial predators suffer greatly regardless of when the damage is discovered. What does differ is the amount of damage done to each type of victim, and the cleanup effort required.

The child victim designation means that somewhere from birth to eighteen years of age, a child was targeted by a thief and successfully robbed of their identity. The adult/juvenile victim is similar to a child victim if he or she was targeted, as well, at some point between birth and eighteen years of age and robbed of their identity. The distinction between the two types of victim is found at the point of discovery. To be a "child" victim means that your parents or guardians discovered that you were a victim of the crime while you were still a juvenile. In other words, before you turned eighteen years old, someone found out through some means that a thief had stolen and used your identity.

In the case of an adult/juvenile victim, the child was victimized at some point from birth to eighteen years of age, but his or her identity theft was not discovered at any point during their youth. It was not until the child became an adult that, through some process, he or she found out they had been victimized. The process I am referring to may include being overlooked for a job, being turned down for credit, being refused a security clearance, being denied entry into college, or being arrested for a crime he or she did not commit. These are a few examples of how an adult/juvenile victim discovers he or she was victimized.

The discovery of victimization is the most critical factor in child identity theft. The attraction of child identity theft versus identity theft of adults is in the amount of time you have to use the identity before the victim ends the criminal's run of wealth, crime, or terror. The most sought-after identity is that of an infant, especially an infant who dies before the deceased child's parents or guardians obtain a Social Security number.

Stealing the identity of a child gives a criminal up to eighteen years to apply for credit cards and home loans, commit crimes, obtain jobs, and exist in our society under the name of your child. Smart thieves know that discovery will be found in the mistakes they make. If they never use your true address, it will be hard for creditors to find parents or guardians, and, therefore, even harder to find the child. Smart thieves know that it is best to steal an identity on the go. In other words, steal as you move to another city or state, or steal and sell to undocumented workers who move across the United States.

Smart parents and guardians ignore credit agencies and others who say to wait until children turn sixteen or eighteen years of age to check their child's credit history. Experts who understand child identity theft know that credit agencies are the problem in this situation. The credit agencies' inability to devise a system that will track all Americans from birth, instead of accepting the first credit application they receive as the truth, is a significant problem.

Credit reporting agencies know they must, by law, provide one credit report for free each year and do not want millions of parents taking advantage of this by asking for one on their children. Do your child a favor and request a free credit report for your child now. Quick action will save both you and your child a lot of additional cleanup if child identity theft is caught in its infancy stages.

QUESTION #55: WHAT SHOULD I TELL CREDITORS IF I SUSPECT MY CHILD'S IDENTITY HAS BEEN STOLEN?

The best advice I can give you is that you are not alone in this embarrassing task you are undertaking. I say this because it happens so frequently that each credit reporting agency, credit card business, banking institution, and mortgage lender has a fraud department. You will obviously want to contact the appropriate creditors if you suspect your child is a victim of identity theft so each can flag the account and reject any future charges.

When you call the agency or business, ask specifically for the fraud department and a fraud investigator. Describing several times to several people what has happened is a waste of your time and effort. Once you speak with a fraud investigator, record his or her name and direct telephone number in your journal or log book for future reference. If the fraud representative is able to assign you a case number, make sure to log the case number for future reference, as well.

Tell the fraud investigator that you are the parent or guardian of a child who received a bill in his or her name that reflects monies owed. If a bill was not received, but rather a credit report revealed the erroneous information, advise the investigator that you discovered the opened account on a credit report in the name of your child. Your phone conversation with the fraud investigator at the company you contacted should deal directly with the credit report entry involving their specific business, or with the bill received from their organization. They will not be able to assist you with any amounts owed with other businesses or organizations. You will need to repeat this process with each creditor who reports erroneous information on your child's credit report. Always remember to keep details of your conversation in your identity theft journal or log book.

Your main discussion point when speaking with someone who thinks your child owes them money is that your child is of an age that makes him or her incapable of incurring the debt supposedly owed. If you give them any daylight of belief that your child possibly did incur the debt because they might be sixteen years old, for example, the creditor will be less likely to help you. Be adamant.

Now is a good time to mention documentation of delivery. Any item that a creditor requests you send to their company should be sent via certified mail or some type of private delivery or courier service that is able to provide you with a recipient's signature and delivery confirmation receipt. While this might be inconvenient, it will certainly enhance your record keeping and hold agencies accountable down the road. I will also add that this extra step taken by you to secure potentially critical evidence will impress your law enforcement officer and legal team, should the documentation need to be presented in court. When you send anything to a creditor, make sure to document it in your child identity theft journal or log book.

When you converse with the creditor or business, do not let them be the only one asking questions. This puts you on the defense. Take an offensive position and ask who, within their organization, took the credit application. When did they take credit or identifying information? Are you allowed to obtain a copy of all paperwork filled out for proof of signature? If the person you are speaking with tells you that you cannot have a copy, ask him or her for the name of the contact person to whom your attorney can send a subpoena.

Record all conversations with creditors and businesses in your journal or log book. Keep records in your accordion folder or, if it gets too large to maintain, a binder. Keep specific sections of records together that deal with one business or company. For example, if your child has a mortgage reported as originated by an out-of-state lender, in addition to a few credit cards in your hometown, keep each company filed separately for quick and easy access of pertinent information. Each entry and debt must be cleared as a separate transaction on the credit report.

Be careful what you send to someone requiring proof of your child's age. As an example, you can make your situation worse by making a copy of a birth certificate, mailing it to someone who may not have any identity theft protective measures in place, and open yourself up to identity theft again. Ask anyone who requests a copy of a birth certificate if there are alternative proof measures. For example, if you are dealing with a mortgage-related identity theft issue, can you take your documentation to a local bank branch and get the branch manager to confirm that your child's birth certificate is certified by your state as authentic instead of sending the requested copy out in the mail? If you cannot, can you get a letter from the institution stating that they will be responsible for the information received and ensure the security of the data?

QUESTION #56: WHAT SHOULD I DO IF I AM CONTACTED BY THE INTERNAL REVENUE SERVICE CONCERNING MY CHILD AND TAX ISSUES?

In February of 2012, the Associated Press published an article in which they said that 24 percent of the 279,000 identity theft claims received by the Federal Trade Commission (FTC) in 2011 involved Social Security numbers stolen and used in filing for fraudulent tax refunds, or used in obtaining employment in occupations the original Social Security number owner never occupied.[1] The FTC reported that this was an increase of 8 percent over the previous year.

To make matters worse, the Associated Press article states that the claims only worsened in 2012 with the number of complaints being filed with the FTC, increasing thus far from 35,000 to 50,000 per week. The majority of the increase is reportedly due to tax and wage identity theft. With identity theft and the theft of Social Security numbers for undocumented workers on the rise, this problem is only going to get worse.

According to the Internal Revenue Service (IRS), a child identity thief uses stolen Social Security numbers for profit in an attempt to scam the government. The scam involves the theft of your child's information to file a tax return claiming a fraudulent refund. The IRS claims that this is usually done early in the tax season so the thief can get it in before the real taxpayer files his or her own return, and receive the refund. When the real taxpayer files, they will be flagged.

You may have a young adult who works a part-time job on the weekends or afternoons after school. If this scam happens to your child, you will receive a notice from the IRS stating that two returns have been submitted using the same Social Security number. Look for the contact telephone number and highlight it. Next, grab a notebook and start your journal or log book. There is a very strong possibility your child has been victimized.

The refund scam is but one problem you might encounter. Another might be a letter from the IRS stating that you have a bill due with penalties for wages that were earned in a previous year and not reported until now by the employer. In other words, your child earned wages and did not file a return because someone used your child's Social Security number.

IRS problems need attention immediately. If not addressed immediately, the process to clear up your child's name with the agency may be very complicated. Do two things as soon as possible. First, look for a point-of-contact name and phone number and make an outbound call to the IRS right away. Second, fill out an IRS Identity Theft Affidavit Form 14039. To obtain this form, go to the IRS website at www.irs.gov. If you report your issue to the IRS and do not receive resolution, call the IRS Identity Protection Specialized Unit at (800) 908-4490. Provide the IRS representative with the claim number and ask him or her the status of your claim. Record all information discussed in your identity theft journal or log book.

The IRS understands the constant scams that thieves attempt daily. Their website has a posted warning to the public advising them that the IRS does not send e-mails requesting your personal information.

The IRS publishes the following helpful documents concerning identity theft:

- Publication 4535 Identity Theft Protection and Victim Assistance
- Publication 4524 Security Awareness—Identity Flyer
- Publication 4523 Beware of Phishing Scheme

IRS Tax Form 911 is a request for taxpayer advocate service assistance. The advocate service assistance is an independent organization within the IRS to assist taxpayers. If you are experiencing harm and economic suffering, use the advocate service to help you.

QUESTION #57: DO I NEED TO HIRE AN ATTORNEY?

Hiring a lawyer is a personal decision. This decision must be made after careful consideration of your specific circumstances. Many situations can be resolved by making phone calls and writing letters. Other circumstances can be resolved once you file a police report. Some situations can even be resolved by taking your child to a bank or lender with their birth certificate to show the bank what a horrible financial decision the company has made by lending money or issuing credit to the fraudster.

There are situations, though, in which an attorney may be helpful or necessary to address legal matters. It could be that you have partial resolution to a theft situation, but you cannot get full clearance of your child's name. In most cases, the main reasons or situations in which an attorney may be helpful are handling court actions, dealing with debt collectors, and resolving Internal Revenue Service issues. In these cases, the issues are so overwhelming that it will take an attorney to help you sift through the legalities and court actions.

You are welcome to research the issue on the web. You will find many opinions on whether an attorney is needed in an identity theft case. The decision is yours as a parent, but I recommend that you take advantage of what our laws have designated as free to you before you expend the cost of hiring an attorney who will charge you to possibly obtain information you can research on your own.

I have previously detailed for you that federal law mandates that the credit reporting agencies provide to each person one free credit report per calendar year. You can hire an attorney to call or write to the credit agency to request a credit report be issued on your behalf, but it is not necessary. Before you finish describing what you need to an attorney, you could have finished the phone call to a credit reporting agency and already have your free credit report on the way to your home. The other free service is a ninety-day credit alert. A credit alert is free and can be set up on your report with a simple phone call to a credit agency. For added theft protection, you may also request a credit freeze be placed on your report. This prohibits anyone from seeing your credit report information without your consent. Unlike a ninety-day credit alert, a credit freeze, is most cases, may be associated with a small fee.

So at what point will I know, in my dealings with businesses, that I have enough concern to need legal representation? As previously mentioned, when you receive a court legal action notice from a sheriff's deputy or police officer, this means that a court date has already been set and legal action has begun. You cannot waste a scheduled court date trying to appear on your own with documents the court may or may not accept. For this issue alone, you need to seek legal representation immediately upon receiving any legal notice.

An attorney can file motions with the court to have the charges dismissed. They can file briefs setting forth the reasons for the requested dismissal. They can request subpoenas of individuals who might not want to testify, or for documents that businesses previously would not provide to you. Attorneys can request continuances on court dates that are too near to properly prepare your child's defense.

An attorney is needed if the first correspondence your child receives from the IRS is a notice to appear in front of a hearing officer or to appear in the federal district court. An attorney can interface with the IRS for you and represent your interests. The attorney can also appear with you and help the court understand your child's dilemma.

I recommend an attorney anytime you have a debt collector hounding you. It is very unlikely the debt collector will stop after the first contact, as most couldn't care less about your situation; they just want their money. Expect debt collectors to call your home, your work, your cell, your relatives, and your friends. The threat of legal action, or the actual filing of legal action against these businesses, is your relief.

QUESTION #58: WHAT DO I NEED TO KNOW ABOUT CREDIT REPORTING AGENCIES?

The first question to answer is, what is a credit reporting agency? The financial world refers to credit bureaus as "credit reporting agencies." A credit reporting agency is a company that collects information on consumers to establish or determine creditworthiness. The basis of what is being determined is, how much of a risk are you? How well do you repay debts? What legal actions have been taken against you to collect amounts owed? Have you filed for bankruptcy? Is there a tax lien against your property?

Credit reporting agencies receive information from banks, credit card companies, mortgage lenders, utility companies, debt collectors, state courts, federal courts, and creditors, such as department stores. The federal government has two agencies responsible for regulation of the credit reporting industry. Oversight for credit reporting agencies comes from the FTC. The oversight for all national banks, who furnish credit agencies with information, is the Office of the Comptroller of Currency (OCC).

For reference purposes, the contact information for the above-mentioned federal agencies is as follows:

The Federal Trade Commission
600 Pennsylvania Avenue
Washington, D.C. 20580
Telephone Number: (202) 326-2222
Website: www.ftc.gov

The Office of the Comptroller of Currency (OCC)
Telephone Number: (202) 874-5000
Website: www.occ.treas.gov/

Formal written complaints with the OCC regarding a national bank or its operating subsidiary should be mailed to:

Customer Assistance Group
1301 McKinney Street
Suite 3450
Houston, TX 77010

Freedom of Information Act (FOIA) Request mailing address:
Comptroller of the Currency
Disclosure Officer
Mail Stop 3-2
Washington, D.C. 20219

General Correspondence to OCC mailing address:
Comptroller of the Currency
Administrator of National Banks
Washington, D.C. 20219

Oversight and regulation is imperative, because the credit reporting agencies are private companies. According to Wikipedia, the five credit reporting agencies are "for-profit businesses and possess no government affiliation."[2] Covered in this book are the three major credit reporting agencies, Experian, Equifax, and TransUnion, though it is worth noting there are two other less recognizable agencies, Innovis and PRBC.

A credit score is established from the records kept by credit reporting agencies. Credit scores are used by credit card companies, banks, mortgage lenders, and other creditors to determine if you are worth the risk in lending money or purchasing power. A good credit score means that you will most likely receive a loan, mortgage, or credit card. A bad score means that you will probably not.

A child should not have a credit report, because they have not established credit. If someone establishes credit in a child's stolen name, then a credit report is generated. As the child's parent, you can obtain a copy of any report on your child. Just contact one of the credit reporting agencies and follow the suggested process below to request a credit report. I also suggest you obtain one for yourself at the same time you request one for your child.

QUESTION #59: HOW CAN I OBTAIN MY CHILD'S CREDIT REPORT?

According to the FTC's website, the Fair Credit Reporting Act (FCRA) requires each of the nationwide consumer reporting agencies to provide you with a free copy of your credit report, at your request, once every twelve months. The major credit agencies are Equifax, Experian, and TransUnion. The federal agency responsible for enforcement of the FCRA is the FTC.

Now that you know what a credit reporting agency is and who and what regulates them, let's look at obtaining your child's report. You can get your free credit report by following the instructions listed below. Most research will tell you that there are three main credit agencies, but there are actually five, as referenced in the last section. Innovis and PRBC are not reported as one of the three major reporting agencies on the FTC website; therefore, I have chosen not to include their information.

Below you will find the contact information for the three major credit reporting agencies:

- Equifax—www.equifax.com
- Experian—www.experian.com
- TransUnion—www.transunion.com

TransUnion—This credit reporting agency has the best-explained system for reporting and requesting child identity theft credit reports. I encourage you to visit their website and complete their online, secure Child Identity Theft Inquiry form. If you have trouble locating it, then type the words "child identity theft inquiry form" in their search block. You will be able to complete the inquiry online for instant submission.

Experian—This credit reporting agency requires you to complete their request form via hard copy and then mail it in for processing. Parents and guardians need to review the submission instructions on Experian's website carefully before mailing a request for a child's credit report due to specific documentation requirements. If your child has a credit file, Experian will provide you with a copy. Armed with a report to review, you can notify the agency via certified mail, return receipt requested, advising them of what information is fraudulent. The Experian website contains a statement that they will not accept faxed documents as a secure means of establishing identification.

Equifax—This credit reporting agency is similar to Experian in that it requires you to complete a credit report inquiry form in hard copy format via mail delivery service.

Each of the credit reporting agencies offers you services you can select or pay for if you desire. The choice is yours, but I encourage you to take advantage of the one free credit report each year you are entitled to by federal law mandate. For this reason alone, you should not be paying for an annual credit report. To ensure you are not charged, visit www.annualcreditreport.com.

Beware of sites that offer free credit monitoring or free credit scores. Sites that offer you free services may end up costing you, as their "free" period may be short in duration and their charges may be recurring on your credit card. Any site that requires your credit card information is not free.

You should also be aware of imposter websites. These are sites that will purposely misspell a web address, tricking you into their website to scam you. If you desire a free credit report as intended by the law, type www.annualcreditreport.com into your web browser. Do not do a web engine search, as this may redirect you to a site you do not desire to visit.

If you receive an offer, pop-up ad, or phone call from someone reporting that he or she is a representative calling on behalf of www.annualcreditreport.com, or any of the three nationwide reporting companies, do not reply. According to the FTC website, this is most likely a scam. If you receive an e-mail you suspect is fraudulent or a scam, forward it immediately to the FTC at spam@uce.gov.

QUESTION #60: WHAT ARE MY RIGHTS REGARDING WHAT IS IN MY CHILD'S CREDIT FILE, AND HOW CAN I CORRECT ERRORS?

As noted earlier, parents have the right to review their child's credit file. This section will further explain how you have the right to obtain documents relating to fraudulent transactions. Businesses and creditors must give you proof of transactions, such as applications and other transaction documents they have. Your request must be in writing and be accompanied by a police report, verification of your identity, and possibly an affidavit (if required).

To recognize errors on your credit report you must first know exactly what is allowed to be in your report. Some of the reporting data will surprise you. Your credit report is actually a credit history for you as an individual. The history is created from a vast number of reporting sources. If you obtain credit from a business, person, or organization, they have the right to report your timeliness of payments to a credit bureau.

Information that you should expect to see on your report is bank loan payments, mortgage payments, vehicle loan payments, and credit card payments. Items reported that you might not be aware of are landlord payments and medical bills from doctors, hospitals, dentists, or specialists. Payment records are also received from utility companies, child support administrators, and items that are of public record, such as bankruptcies, civil judgments, and tax liens.

Your report will contain your name and any name variation you may have used in the past, your current and previous address information, and all employment information known to the credit agency. A little-known fact is that in addition to everything listed above, your report can, under the authority granted in the Fair Credit Reporting Act, also list known crime convictions. Most credit agencies do not report crime convictions as a matter of practice, but they may in connection with an employer background check, insurance company application, or an application to rent a home, condominium, or apartment.

Now that you know what is in the report, you should learn what your rights are. You have the right to know who has been checking on your credit. Any company or individual who checks your credit information will be listed as a credit inquiry on your report. When you receive your credit report, it should automatically list who has inquired about your credit during the last six months.

Once you receive your report, you need to know that one in four credit reports has invalid data on it serious enough to be considered critical or serious errors. How do these errors occur? You could have been mistaken for someone else, and the data was entered on the wrong person's credit history. You might also have the same name as another person who is not making their payments on time.

In child identity theft cases, virtually any information on a credit report under your child's name is an error. Remember, your child is not supposed to have a credit report yet unless he or she is out in the workforce and engaging in credit-related services. Review the credit report for accuracy. If you find errors, you need to dispute them.

How do you dispute an error? Write the credit reporting agency a letter advising them exactly what you desire to dispute. They have thirty days to investigate what you dispute. Ask them to produce documents with signatures. A critical note is that the credit reporting agency must be able to verify the negative information they have received from the business, person, or organization, and if they cannot, they must remove the information from the credit report. Once all disputed items are removed from the corrected credit report, you are entitled to a free copy of the corrected report.

What happens if you get another credit report in six months or a year and the information you thought you had corrected reappears? Federal laws require credit reporting agencies to notify you in writing within five days of reinserting any information previously removed. When doing so, the credit agencies must provide you with a toll-free telephone number to dispute the information being reinserted and give you the opportunity to dispute it.

QUESTION #61: HOW CAN I BLOCK IDENTITY THEFT–RELATED INFORMATION FROM SHOWING UP ON MY CHILD'S CREDIT REPORT?

If your child's credit report contains information that was the result of identity theft, you have the right to request that the credit agency block it from your credit file. To accomplish this, you must, as part of the process of reporting, call the police and have a police agency investigate your child identity theft case. Armed with a police report, the credit reporting agencies are required to investigate, and if appropriate, remove the fraudulent data entries.

The following is an excerpt from the Fair Credit Reporting Act as it pertains to blocking information on your child's credit report that was placed there as the result of identity theft:

The Fair Credit Reporting Act
§ 605B. Block of information resulting from identity theft [15 U.S.C. §1681c-2]

(a) *Block.* Except as otherwise provided in this section, a consumer reporting agency shall block the reporting of any information in the file of a consumer that the consumer identifies as information that resulted from an alleged identity theft, not later than 4 business days after the date of receipt by such agency of –

(1) appropriate proof of the identity of the consumer;

(2) a copy of an identity theft report;

(3) the identification of such information by the consumer; and

(4) a statement by the consumer that the information is not information relating to any transaction by the consumer.

(b) *Notification.* A consumer reporting agency shall promptly notify the furnisher of information identified by the consumer under subsection (a)--

(1) that the information may be a result of identity theft;

(2) that an identity theft report has been filed;

(3) that a block has been requested under this section; and

(4) of the effective dates of the block.[3]

If in the process of checking your child's report you check yours as well and find fraudulent or erroneous information, you have the right to ask the credit bureau to notify any company who has pulled your credit within the last six months to be notified of the concern. You can also request that anyone who received a credit report containing the erroneous information be sent another credit report once corrected. While your child does not need the credit at an early age, you need the best credit score possible for potential future borrowing needs.

The FTC also has a complaint process that assists you in gathering information in a report to give to the police and creditors. Go to www.ftc

.gov, go to their "Consumer Protection" folder, and click on the "complaint assistant." The complaint assistant is a web-based reporting form that captures your child's identity theft issue. This form is printable and can be attached to the police report you obtain from your local or state police when you report the crime. Reporting identity theft to the FTC also assists the commission in capturing identity theft as it occurs across the United States.

You now have the information to review your child's credit report and block information that should not be there. Any information needing to be purged should be requested, investigated, and removed. The law is on your side.

QUESTION #62: WHAT IS A FRAUD ALERT, AND WHEN SHOULD I PLACE ONE ON MY CHILD'S CREDIT FILE?

Identity theft costs our economy over 60 billion dollars every year. Child identity theft is the leader among all identity theft crimes when it comes to repeat offenses against the same victim. Child identity theft also leads in the category of length of time a criminal has to commit an identity theft crime against the victim.

The original system of fraud alerts was probably developed for adults before criminals figured out the rewards of stealing a child's creditworthy information. The system today benefits children far more than it does adults. The reason for this is that children do not check their credit reports annually; therefore, they are more susceptible to undiscovered identity theft.

Adults have the upper hand when it comes to being able to discover identity theft. Adults have established monthly billing cycles and established creditors they do business with. They are also connected with the services of the business world and are easily traceable for bill collectors. Having said all the above, however, the average time of discovery for an adult involved in an identity theft scam is approximately fourteen months. Nine to eighteen percent of adult victims take four years or longer to discover that they have been victimized by identity theft criminals.

These statistics are sad when you consider that adults have the ability to get a free credit report check once every twelve months. Parents who get involved in the prevention of child identity theft can, as a by-product, protect themselves as well. They can also educate other relatives, explaining the benefit of child identity theft education. Learning the definition of an alert and the benefit an alert can bring you is a great place to start.

A fraud alert is a notice and warning to anyone looking at your child's credit file that your child is a potential victim of identity theft. This alert is a notice to anyone who is considering issuing credit in your name that you will be contacted prior to credit issuance. Fraud alerts may require you to provide a phone number so anyone planning to issue credit can call you for verification if they desire (not mandatory). All fraud alerts are free and can be initiated by calling any one of the three major credit reporting agencies (Equifax, Experian, or TransUnion).

A fraud alert is considered a first step in the process of protecting your credit, and a great idea when you, as a parent or guardian, suspect your child may have been victimized. Whether you have started receiving credit card offers in your child's name, or your phone is ringing with debt collectors, the initial credit alert is one of your best measures to reduce further fraud. It is a great tool to protect your child during the interim period of suspecting child identity theft and receiving that credit report that tells you exactly what has happened in your child's name.

Alerts come in several different varieties. The first is a ninety-day alert. This is also often referred to as an initial alert. Initial alerts are quick and easy to place on your child's credit file but expire in ninety days. The good news is that each ninety days you are allowed to reactivate the alert if needed.

Active duty alerts are for active duty military members and provide them with the same benefits that the initial alert does. The benefit of an active duty alert for military members is that it does not require reactivation every ninety days. The active duty military alert protects military members for twelve months. Extended alerts are available for severe cases and last for seven years. Extended alerts require law enforcement involvement and are allowed in cases where victims' identities are sold and resold, causing repeated identity theft.

QUESTION #63: HOW LONG SHOULD I KEEP AN ALERT ON MY CHILD'S CREDIT FILE?

A fraud alert needs to remain on your child's credit file until you are sure there is no longer an increased threat of identity theft. In other words, ask yourself what it was that caused you to request that a credit alert be placed on the file in the first place, and has that issue been resolved? If so, you can remove the alert, allow it to remain, and elect not to renew it when it expires. It is important to note, though, you may ask that it be renewed if your concerns remain.

There are multiple types of credit file alerts: initial alerts, active duty alerts for military personnel, extended alerts, and credit freezes. If you feel you have been victimized and desire to have a fraud alert placed on your file, any one agency (Equifax, Experian, or TransUnion) notified will contact the other two and advise them of the alert. You do not need to contact all three credit reporting agencies, with one exception. Innovis, according to their website, does not share credit reporting information with Equifax, Experian, or TransUnion; thus, you must contact one of the three agencies mentioned above, plus Innovis, to ensure you are covered with all agencies.

Initial alerts are alerts placed on a credit file by a consumer. An individual consumer, or a representative acting on behalf of the consumer, such as a parent or guardian, can request a fraud alert. This alert is placed on a child's file based on the fact that you suspect he or she has been, or is about to become, the victim of an identity-related crime. Once you place the alert, it is good for ninety days. Leave it on the file and allow it to protect your child until the ninety-day period runs out. At the end of ninety days, it must be renewed. If the issue has been resolved, then great, but if not, then renewal is an option.

If you feel the need to place an alert on your child's credit file, I suggest you take the proactive measure of putting your home phone number, as well as each family member's cell phone number, on the government's Do Not Call Registry. To register your phone numbers on the Do Not Call Registry, go to www.donotcall.gov on the Internet and follow the instructions. This registration will require you to have an e-mail address for verification, but this is a free service and should begin the process of eliminating unwanted calls, solicitors, and harassing sales pitches.

Other considerations a parent or guardian needs to make, if placing a credit alert on a child's file, are what information they have on their computer, what e-mails they have received, and what security settings are in place. Until you know the source of the theft, you, as the parent or guardian, must cover all bases. Check your child's computer for viruses and have him or her report anything suspicious.

Active duty alerts are designed for active duty Army, Air Force, Coast Guard, Marine Corps, and Navy personnel. The active duty alert has the same effects as an initial credit file alert. The duration of an active duty alert is twelve months. Active duty alerts protect service personnel who do not have the ability to frequently update alerts, such as the initial alert.

An extended alert requires that you submit proof, such as an identity theft report, that you have been victimized. Upon receipt of sufficient proof, a fraud alert will be placed on a consumer's file for seven years. During the first five years of the seven-year period, the consumer will be excluded from any list of consumers provided to third parties for credit or insurance offers not initiated by you, the consumer. Extended alerts entitle the consumer to more protection for a longer period of time. This includes two free credit file disclosures in a twelve-month period.

Initial, active duty, and extended alerts can be canceled by the consumer at any time. Current laws and policies that govern alerts are subject to change as well. For the latest information and updates on fraud alerts, please visit the FTC website at www.ftc.gov.

QUESTION #64: WHAT IS A CREDIT FREEZE, AND UNDER WHAT CIRCUMSTANCES SHOULD I ASK FOR ONE FOR MY CHILD?

A credit freeze prohibits the issuance of any further credit in your child's name, or the use of his or her Social Security number without first contacting you. A credit freeze is more of a permanent step in stopping credit issuance. Credit freezes are sometimes referred to as security freezes.

As just stated, the credit freeze prohibits the issuance of credit without first contacting you. To issue credit, the credit reporting agency must obtain your authorization to lift the freeze either temporarily or permanently. Most credit agencies have the information on their website for obtaining a credit freeze. Upon receipt, the credit agency will issue you a letter containing a confirmation number. To lift the freeze, you must be able to provide the confirmation number when contacted.

A credit freeze is more complicated than a fraud alert. I encourage you to view each credit reporting agency's website for their required information and process. A credit freeze would be appropriate for a child who has had their identity stolen and sold to undocumented workers. Freezing your credit does not affect your credit rating. It does not prevent you from obtaining your free credit report.

For more information on credit freezing, contact the following credit reporting agencies:

- Equifax—www.equifax.com
- Experian—www.experian.com
- TransUnion—www.transunion.com

Credit freezes differ greatly from credit alerts. A credit freeze is good only for the credit agency to which you apply. This means that you must correspond with each credit agency independently and go through the same process to fully protect your child. Credit freezes can be temporary or permanent. Once you place the freeze on the file, it is up to you to follow up and remove the freeze from the file.

In adult identity theft cases, credit freezes can be an inconvenience because they stop the issuance of credit. Make sure you have researched this thoroughly before you do it, because it does limit your ability to get quick access to credit; your child does not need it, but you might if you are the victim instead of your child. If you are the victim, ensure that the credit reporting agency has your cell or home phone number so they can call you when either you or someone else applies for credit in your name.

If you are concerned about a credit freeze affecting a current account you have open, do not worry. Credit freezes do not affect accounts that already exist. They also do not affect parties that may have access to your file unrelated to new accounts, such as law enforcement officers and some government agencies for reasons of investigation or a statutory responsibility.

Credit freezes are not necessarily free. If you view the credit reporting agencies' websites, you will see that different states have different prices. For example, the fees range from no cost to $20 on the TransUnion website. Typically victims can place the freeze for free. If you have not been victimized by identity theft and you still desire to place a freeze on your credit file, you may experience a fee. The services are the same whether you are being charged a fee or not.

QUESTION #65: HOW CAN I CLEAR MY CHILD'S NAME?

Clearing your child's name is one of the most challenging parts of the process, since it requires patience, persistence, and careful record keeping. Documentation will be your best friend. Logical step reporting will assist you greatly. To assist you further, I have created a checklist that you can use as a guide:

- ❏ Create a journal or log book.
- ❏ File a complaint with the FTC.
- ❏ Initiate a credit alert with a credit reporting agency.
- ❏ Request a credit report for your child from a credit reporting agency.
- ❏ Request a credit report for other family members as a proactive measure.
- ❏ Contact the police (local department, local precinct, county sheriff's office, county police department, parish sheriff's office, state police, state patrol, state bureau of criminal investigation, or state highway patrol).
- ❏ If the child identity theft involves terrorism, did you contact the FBI?
- ❏ If the child identity theft involves phishing or a computer scam, have you saved all copies of e-mails?
- ❏ If the child identity theft involved a military dependent ID, did you contact the military police?

❑ If the child identity theft involves the U.S. mail, did you contact your U.S. postal inspector?

❑ Obtain a copy of the police report.

❑ If the child identity theft involves a lost or stolen passport, file a form DS64 with the Department of State.

❑ If the child identity theft involved a tax return or reported income, contact the IRS.

❑ Contact creditors who issued credit in your child's name.

❑ Notify your bank that a family member has been the victim of child identity theft in case a garbage thief stole information from more than one family member.

❑ Request a benefits and earnings statement from the Social Security Administration.

❑ If your child identity theft involved medical information, contact your insurance company.

❑ If the child identity theft involved a vehicle purchase or driver's license, has the department or division of motor vehicles been notified?

❑ If the child identity theft involved your child's cell phone number, contact the cell phone provider.

❑ If the child identity theft involved government assistance, has the appropriate agency been notified?

❑ If the child identity theft involved disaster relief, has FEMA been notified?

❑ Advise your child's school and doctor that your child's information has been compromised and that you must approve any information released until further notice.

❑ Ensure your family's phone numbers are listed on the Do Not Call Registry.

❑ Contact an attorney (optional).

❑ Do you have required court dates to attend?

❑ Does your child need counseling as a result of the child identity theft?

There may be other items you could add to this list. If so, make a notation in your journal or log book to ensure you follow up on the added issues.

QUESTION #66: HOW DID WE GET SOCIAL SECURITY NUMBERS IN THE FIRST PLACE?

Trivia 101: In what year was the first Social Security number developed, and who contracted with the Social Security Administration (SSA) to distribute and assign the first batch of Social Security numbers? If you miraculously answered 1936 and the U.S. Post Office, then you are correct. In 1935, the Social Security Act (P.L. 74-271) was enacted, authorizing the creation of a record-keeping system.

In November of 1936, the SSA sent the first SS-4 application forms to employers via the U.S. postal distribution process. Using the data collected from employers, the postal offices then supplied an SS-5 form for employees to complete. The U.S. Postal Service had been selected because it maintained 45,000 offices across America, 1,074 of which were large enough to be designated as "typing centers."

When employees completed the SS-5 form, they had the option to hand deliver it to their mail carrier or visit the typing center for their new Social Security card. Once completed, all records of the issuance of the Social Security card were sent to the SSA headquarters in Baltimore. Once there, the records were grouped in blocks of 1,000 and the master records created.

"On December 1, 1936, the first block of 1,000 records were assembled and were ready to start their way through the nine-step process that would result in the creation of a permanent master record and the establishment of an earnings record for the individual."[4] This record included a card issued to each individual worker. The card they would receive was designed by Fred Happel of Albany, New York. Happel was commissioned by the SSA to develop three designs to be considered. He was paid $60 for his work, which became the first card used by the SSA.

In 1962, the Internal Revenue Service adopted the Social Security number as their official method of tracking taxpaying citizens. In 1969, the Department of Defense changed their system of identifying service personnel from military service numbers to the Social Security number.

Since 1936, society has changed greatly, but what has remained consistent is the system of Social Security numbers. Social Security numbers continue to be the method for the government to track wages and earnings.

Unfortunately, criminals who use identity theft as their tool have abused this great mechanism.

While child identity theft is a new-age crime, the most misused individual Social Security number of all time is not new, but rather quite old. In 1938, wallet manufacturer E. H. Feree of Lockport, New York, decided to promote his product by showing how a Social Security card would fit easily into one of his new-for-sale products. He included in each of the wallets that was sold a card that looked just like a real Social Security card and had the number 078-05-1120 on it.

This sample card was meant for display purposes, and while each new wallet contained one, it was not meant to be a real Social Security card. The company vice president decided that it would be a clever idea to use the Social Security number of his secretary, which he did. This wallet was sold in Woolworth stores all across America. Even though it was a bit smaller than an actual card and was printed in red with the word "specimen" on it, the card was misused often in fraud.

In the peak year of 1943, 5,755 people were using the Social Security number of Feree's secretary, and in all over 40,000 people have been found to have used the number. In 1977, twelve people were found to still be using that same Social Security number issued by Feree. Identity theft is a continuing crime that has been around for many years and will continue to be, as evidenced by this example.

QUESTION #67: WHAT IS AN "AREA" NUMBER, AND HOW DOES IT AFFECT MY CHILD?

Area numbers are the first three numbers in a Social Security number issued to your child by the SSA prior to 2011. A child's Social Security number consisted of nine numbers containing area numbers, group numbers, and personal identifiers. The first three numbers in the Social Security number were assigned by the geographical region that you lived in.

When the system was first developed, the government started issuing area numbers, giving the states in the Northeast theirs first, then moving west-

Table 4.1. Social Security Administration Area Numbers

Alabama 416–424	Nebraska 505–508
Alaska 574	Nevada 530
American Samoa 586	New Hampshire 001–003
Arizona 526–527, 600–601	New Jersey 135–158
Arkansas 429–432	New Mexico 525, 585
California 545–573, 602–626	New York 050–134
Colorado 521–524	North Carolina 237–246, 232
Connecticut 040–049	North Dakota 501–502
Delaware 221–222	Ohio 268–302
Washington, D.C. 577–579	Oklahoma 440–448
Florida 261–267, 589–595	Oregon 540–544
Georgia 252–260	Pennsylvania 159–211
Guam 586	Puerto Rico 580
Hawaii 575–576	Rhode Island 035–039
Idaho 518–519	South Carolina 247–251
Illinois 318–361	South Dakota 503–504
Indiana 303–317	Tennessee 408–415
Iowa 478–485	Texas 449–467
Kansas 509–515	Utah 528–529
Kentucky 400–407	Vermont 008–009
Louisiana 433–439	Virginia 223–231
Maine 004–007	Virgin Islands 580
Maryland 212–220	Washington 531–539
Massachusetts 010–034	West Virginia 232–236
Michigan 362–386	Wisconsin 387–399
Minnesota 468–477	Wyoming 520
Mississippi 425–428, 587, 588	Railroad Retirement Board 700–728
Missouri 486–500	Outside the U.S. 586
Montana 516–517	

Source: Social Security Administration Bulletin, November 1982/Vol. 45, No. 11. 2012. Accessed April 5, 2012. www.ssa.gov/policy/docs/ssb/v45n11/v45n11p29.pdf.

ward. That is why numbers issued in the East are lower than those issued in the West. Table 4.1 provides a list of area numbers across America as published by the SSA.

Area numbers were just one piece of predictable information a child identity thief needed to steal your child's financial future. Following area numbers were group numbers and serial numbers in the sequence. Armed with each of these three groups of numbers, a thief could assume the identity of your child.

QUESTION #68: WHAT ARE "GROUP" NUMBERS AND "SERIAL" NUMBERS, AND HOW DO THEY AFFECT MY CHILD?

Social Security numbers issued, prior to 2011's randomization, had two middle numbers within the nine-number sequence called group numbers. Group numbers ranged from 01 to 99. The odd numbers 01 through 09 were issued first, followed by the even numbers 10 through 98. SSA regional offices used to have an allocation of these numbers to issue, but the group number had no special geographic or data signification. The group numbers 00 were not used except for administrative purposes.

Group numbers were simply an administrative convenience for the SSA. They would break them down and give certain portions to different states to use. The group number (which was the fourth and fifth number in the Social Security number) was initially determined by U.S. Post Office locations that made the assignments when the numbering system first began. These post offices were given 10,000 numbers to issue out in their area of responsibility on behalf of the Social Security Board's Bureau of Old-Age Benefits.

Group numbers can be complicated when you try to follow the logic. Before 1965, only half of the group numbers were used. The odd numbers were used below the number 10 and the even numbers were used above the number 9. In 1965, the SSA changed the system. The change in assignments gave us a system of issuing low even numbers and the high odd numbers in the following order:

1. Odd numbers 01 through 09
2. Even numbers 10 through 98
3. Even numbers 02 through 08
4. Odd numbers 11 through 99

This brings us to serial numbers. The last four numbers in your child's Social Security number prior to 2011 were called serial numbers. Serial numbers ranged from 0001 through 9999. Serial numbers were designed to be uniquely assigned to an individual person and not to be repeated. The numbers were issued in consecutive order.

The SSA used to publish a monthly list of the highest group assigned for each Social Security number area. This ceased to exist after June 25, 2011, when the SSA started using "randomization." Randomization is a new method of issuing Social Security numbers.

The SSA claims that it changed to the new system for two reasons. The first was that they were running out of area numbers. The system was exhausting itself. The second was that the Social Security number contained predictable numbers, which led to identity theft and child identity theft. A system of randomization allows the SSA to use certain number series that had previously not been used.

The randomization of numbers eliminates the area number and freezes the high group list that had been used to verify the validity of Social Security numbers. To assist law enforcement, employers, and SSA personnel, the government has created the E-Verify program. The E-Verify program allows an employer, for example, to verify that a Social Security number is valid, is assigned to one particular subject, and that the individual assigned to the number is eligible to work in the United States. Some states require employers to use E-Verify when hiring an employee.

QUESTION #69: WHEN SHOULD I OBTAIN A SOCIAL SECURITY NUMBER FOR MY CHILD?

We just discussed the uniqueness of Social Security numbers; now let's take a moment and talk about when they should be requested from the SSA. Should parents get them at birth or wait until the child gets older? What are your options as a parent or guardian? These are just a few questions we will tackle.

Let's get started with when you should obtain a Social Security number and card for your child. There are two options; the first is to obtain it after birth while still at the hospital, and the second is to wait until a later date you desire before the child turns eighteen years old. Before you decide, consider what you might need the number for. Here are some items for which a child might need a Social Security number:

- Opening a savings account
- Opening an investment account in their name
- Completing a required tax return
- Obtaining a U.S. passport
- Obtaining health insurance
- Obtaining life insurance
- Participating in a prepaid college investment plan
- Buying U.S. savings bonds

The first option is to obtain a child's Social Security number at the hospital. In this case, the hospital will assist you by providing you with the necessary forms when they complete the state birth certificate registration paperwork. If you select this option, the SSA will mail the Social Security card to your address once it is completed. This is the best choice, as registering your child as soon as possible prevents a child identity theft criminal from registering as your child and requesting the number and card before you do. This option prevents a would-be thief from reading the newspaper birth announcement and filing for the number before you do as well.

Once complete, your application will be forwarded to the SSA, then received and processed. The application and issuance process takes approximately twelve weeks. The next option is to obtain a child's Social Security number at a later date. If you elect this as your option, you will need to complete Form SS-5 (Social Security Number Application Request Form) at a later date to obtain the Social Security number. Be prepared to show U.S. citizenship, age, and identity documents for your child. You will also be required to show a document proving your identity.

It is best to submit your application in person. If this is not possible, it is in most cases acceptable to mail your application to your nearest SSA office with either original documents or copies certified by the issuing agency. Your nearest office should be found in the government section of your local phone book, or you can research www.socialsecurity.gov for a convenient location. Once there, click on the tab on the left side of their home page that says "Find a Social Security Office."

It is a good idea to call ahead if you can for office hours and clarification on acceptable documents to take with you. Some metropolitan areas, such as New York City, Las Vegas, Orlando, and Phoenix may require you to appear in person. First-time applicants age twelve or older must apply in person regardless of the location. Even if you appear in person, plan to wait up to twelve weeks before the card is issued, as the SSA needs processing time to verify the documents you have provided.

QUESTION #70: SHOULD I AUTOMATICALLY REQUEST A NEW SOCIAL SECURITY NUMBER FOR MY CHILD AFTER DISCOVERING IDENTITY THEFT?

When adults become victims of identity theft, some of their first phone calls are to credit card companies, banks, and insurance providers. The inevitable request is to cancel the card and issue the victim another one. This is a natural reaction, but one you should reconsider in most cases concerning child identity theft, and specifically, in the case of the Social Security card.

Social Security numbers are assigned as unique personal identifying numbers. They are never issued to more than one person. The ultimate goal of the Social Security number is to record income earned during your lifetime so that benefits can be paid at the retirement eligibility age. Benefits can also be paid on disability claims.

Your goal in reporting abuse to the SSA should be to encourage accurate earnings reporting. If your child has fraudulent earnings on their Social Security benefits and earnings statement, the SSA will assist you with clearing up child identity theft issues and subtracting the fraudulent earnings.

As a general rule, the SSA will ask you the details of your child identity theft to try to figure out if your case is bad enough to require the issuance of a new number. If you have been the victim of repeated use and reuse, you may be a candidate for a new card. An example of repeated use would be a Social Security number that was obtained by an undocumented worker who used the number repeatedly to obtain employment, credit cards, vehicles, and/or a mortgage. If this same child's Social Security number was then resold to other undocumented workers, then the SSA might agree that a new number needs to be issued.

So why won't the SSA give you another number if your child has been victimized once by identity theft? There are several reasons for the cautious stance the SSA has taken with reissuing Social Security numbers. The first reason has to do with the fact that they have had this policy for many years. We have previously discussed that, under the old serialization system, there were concerns about the maximum numbers available before the system of number assignments ran out.

The policies of reissuance of Social Security numbers are the same for both adults and children. The next reissue concern is the impact of affecting multiple personal tracking entities such as the IRS, health and life insurance companies, medical and dental records, school records, savings bonds, and driving records. An important note to make is that the SSA does not make notification to other federal agencies when a child identity theft occurs.

Once a person is recognized and tracked in databases, ensuring full and complete change is challenging. A good example of this is that credit reporting agencies will not combine records issued under different Social Security numbers. The SSA will not void a Social Security number either. What will occur is that the original number will remain assigned to you, with a new number given to you and cross-referenced to the old number. The reason for this policy is that income earned in the years prior to the theft needs to be tracked continuously until benefits are paid.

The SSA will change a child's number if they find out that your child's number was issued in error and that another child or adult already had that same number legitimately issued to them previously. The SSA will also entertain severe abuse cases, life endangerment, or harassment cases. Lastly, the SSA will review cases where the person claims that they have religious or cultural objections to a number assigned, or to the digits within a series of assigned numbers.

QUESTION #71: IF I WORK IN A MEDICAL OFFICE, WHAT CAN I DO TO PROTECT OUR PATIENTS?

Those who work in the medical profession are key in prevention of both identity theft and child identity theft. They work at a location that must have your most personal information to care for you properly. Unfortunately, while they may be great at medical care, seldom are they experts at child identity theft or identity theft. It is okay—law enforcement and this book can help.

If you work for a doctor's office, hospital, dentist's office, orthodontist, elder care facility, emergency clinic, or as a school nurse, you can directly impact the safety of your patients. The first thing you can do is build on your knowledge of child identity theft. Use the information in this book as a guide to make your medical office a harder target for identity thieves.

A good place to start is a review of the security of patient files. Does your office keep them in view of the visitors who come to the front window? If it does, I would ask why. From a law enforcement officer's point of view, keeping a patient file visible at the receptionist's window is like parking a vehicle, locked or unlocked, with a wallet or purse visible in the front seat. Neither is a good idea.

Two things occur; the first is the temptation of having a gold mine of information within sight of an identity thief when he or she walks up to the window. This situation is commonly referred to as an opportunist crime. Opportunistic criminals may or may not take the initiative to commit a crime; however, if the opportunity presents itself, it may be too hard to turn down.

The second occurrence is the confirmation of the exact location of all information. Remember, a child identity thief or identity thief will not break into your medical office to steal drugs. Not all break-ins are discovered in identity theft. Thieves committing this crime will try to get in and steal or copy patient data files, and then neatly replace your data information before leaving. If you do not suspect a break-in, then your patients will never be notified.

Child identity thieves may also try employment with your office or employment with a service provider to your office. Do you have your office cleaned during office hours or does an employee remain to watch the cleaning if done after hours? Does your office have a policy on the accountability of copied patient files? Are you allowed to take "work" home?

Another weakness you can work on is computer information. Do any of your computer screens face patients or visitors? If so, it encourages "shoulder surfing," which is a person being "nosy" by looking over an office worker's shoulder at the computer screen and reading the information. If it is their own record, it may only contain doctor's notes that the employee may not realize the patient will see, but if it is someone else's record, such as a child, it gives pertinent child identity theft information.

Does your office encourage passwords that are complex, unrelated to easy personal information, and include non-alphanumeric characters? Do you change system passwords when an employee leaves your company? Do you screen persons that work on your computers when you have problems? These questions are critical, as your computers contain very personal patient data that, when compromised, can cause significant damage to patients.

A great resource for you is your police department crime prevention officer. Contact your state, local, or sheriff's office and ask to speak with a crime prevention specialist, crime prevention officer, or crime prevention deputy. They can provide you with a crime prevention assessment of the physical security of your building, security survey of your office, and system tips on enhancing your technology security. Take advantage of this resource. In most all cases it will be free and enhance your relationship with law enforcement, providing you with improved preventive information.

QUESTION #72: I WORK IN THE MEDICAL PROFESSION. HELP ME UNDERSTAND MEDICAL IDENTITY THEFT VERSUS CHILD IDENTITY THEFT AND HOW I CAN MAKE A DIFFERENCE.

A very serious problem that plagues child identity theft victims is child medical identity theft. Medical identity theft, committed against children, is the act of someone stealing a child's personal information to obtain medical care under the child's stolen name. Medical identity theft also occurs to obtain needed or desired drugs, or to submit fake billings to insurance companies. Medical identity theft can disrupt a child's life, put their health at risk, and damage their credit rating.

Many dangers exist with this crime, but most center on the mixing of the original patient's information with that of the person using the information. In other words, if I steal your child's information from your family doctor and then visit your local hospital for a medical procedure, the hospital treatment records now have the wrong person's treatment information inserted as your child's.

The secondary concern is insurance fraud. Most child medical identity theft occurs because someone wants medical coverage for the thief's child or relative. Unlike obtaining credit, medical identity theft can only be used for as long as it takes the bills to get to the insurer and insurance client. These parameters tend to make these crimes single-use crimes.

Single-use crimes are those the thief does not intend to use repetitively; they need health care for a specific issue, such as a medical surgical procedure or illness. Children's insurance information may be stolen by anyone with access to that information. Holders of that type of information usually include school workers, medical office workers, day care providers, sports league employees, foster care system employees, friends, or relatives. If you work for a medical office, dental office, or hospital, would you be able to recognize the signs of child medical identity theft? Recognition starts with the receptionist at any location, but must continue throughout all levels of care. Children in need of medical care rarely know their own insurance information. Parents or guardians know whether they have insurance or not and know if the information they have to present for care is stolen.

Patients who visit on a frequent or semifrequent basis will probably be more well-known in the care provider's office. This is why someone attempting child medical identity theft will tend to visit as a new patient or show up at an immediate care facility or hospital emergency room. A child identity thief does not want you to know either them or their children, because the information being presented will not match the truth. They may go to great lengths, including traveling to cities far away from the child they stole the information from.

So as medical team members, how do you recognize medical identity theft? For medical workers such as a doctor's office or hospital, recognition begins with the first person who receives information and continues with each caretaker thereafter. Each member looks for inconsistencies. Each person on the medical team listens for parents who try to explain away information that does not match records. For example, if your hospital record has the child's blood type as O positive but the child seeking care has A negative, this is a red flag.

Red flags will be explained away as mistakes by clerical or medical staff. Mixed blood types will be easy to spot, but different addresses are accepted. Inconsistencies may be cleared up through policies and creativity. When a child is treated, do you require parental identification or just verbal approval and a signature? Help your office understand child identity theft and the different ways it is committed.

Discuss with your staff what systems you have in place to detect inconsistencies. If you have a patient who shows up with inconsistent patient data, how will you deal with it? If your billing reveals inconsistencies, do you follow up on it? If your medical chart information shows inconsistencies, do you address it with the appropriate nurse or doctor? How often do you see things that puzzle you as a nurse or doctor? If an X-ray in your file says that the child patient had a broken bone the last time in, but the child and parent claim they never had an injury, who was the thief—this child or the last one who visited under the same name? The only way to know is to ask questions. When in doubt, insist on further proper identification.

If you have concerns that arise during a patient's visit, contact the police. Because a great deal of medical child identity theft is single usage, police contact at the time of the visit may be the only chance at discovering the real identity of the person attempting to obtain fraudulent care. Your ability to detect this type of fraud may save the real patient's life by preventing a change in the records. Consider, for a moment, the effect of penicillin administered to a child with this allergy; death may be the outcome. Take medical child identity theft seriously.

QUESTION #73: IF MY CHILD HAS BECOME A VICTIM OF MEDICAL IDENTITY THEFT, HOW DO I CORRECT THE MEDICAL RECORDS?

Finding out that your child has been victimized is never easy. Parents feel shock, disbelief, anger, and resentment. Many things complicate the cleanup of child identity theft devastation. Part of the problem with theft of a child's medical information is that you will probably never know if the one location that you find out about was the only incident or if there were more.

Identity thieves usually commit medical identity theft for treatments under coverage of your child's insurance policy. There are, however, cases of child identity theft where your child's identity was stolen for employment and the thief does not need your insurance, just your child's name. When this occurs, the identity may be stolen for the adult thief who needs legalization, or the thief's child who needs the same.

Regardless of the type of child identity theft, or the motive behind the theft, once it has occurred, your child's personal information becomes tangled with another person's. The person to whom your child is linked may have different allergic reactions, be on different medications, have a different blood type, different illnesses, or will have had a completely different medical history. It is rare that two siblings are treated the same medically throughout life, let alone two completely different strangers.

Once you discover your child's medical identity theft, it is imperative that you dedicate time to clearing up any known damage. In addition to cleaning up what has been done, you must ensure that all medical care received in the future is done with the correct information and treatment record. You will have to deal with this hard reality, because the child identity thief may have visited any treatment facility you may visit, and you must ensure that your child's diagnosis relies only upon your child's current situation, information, and past medical history.

If your family has been victimized, contact the police. Ask them to take a report and investigate the crime. Take the time to report the crime on the FTC's website, www.ftc.gov. Once at the website, under the tab "Consumers," click on "Filing a Complaint with the FTC." Having a police report and proof from the FTC will assist you in clearing up child medical identity theft.

Once you have notified the police and filed the FTC report, contact your insurance provider. They can provide information on submitted claims and track future health care submissions. The insurance company's fraud department can also assist the police with the investigation by providing them with information on where the thieves visited, what ailments they claimed, what addresses they reported, phone numbers they reported, and who treated the person submitting themselves as your child.

You should contact one of the three major credit reporting agencies to advise them that your child has been victimized. Request that you need to place a ninety-day credit alert on your child's file. Next you need to contact your child's physician and your child's school. You will probably be unaware of where the data breach occurred, so these entities need to be notified that your child has been victimized and that they need to strengthen the security of their file information.

If you receive bills in relation to the medical identity theft, contact the hospital, doctor, or dentist that sent you the bill. Advise the company from whom you received the bill of the victimization and of the name of the law enforcement officer who is working your child's case. If you receive phone calls from a debt collector, explain the situation and provide a copy of the police report. If you receive civil documents in the mail or from a law enforcement officer stating you owe sums of money, contact an attorney or, if your family is a military family, visit your judge advocate general's office for assistance.

A child will have to be aware he or she is a victim of medical identity theft and possibly deal with it for many years. Knowing this, you may want to consider counseling for your family. There are many types of victimization and many ways to deal with the damage. A professional counselor or therapist can provide your family positive tools to deal with a bad situation, and ensure that each of you has the best chance at emerging with good mental health.

Here are some tips to help you prevent medical identity theft in the future:

- View medical bills for services you did not receive.
- Review insurance statements for double billings for the same service.
- Scrutinize the dates on medical bills for discrepancies.
- View your credit report for bills owed at locations you did not visit.

5

COPING WITH THE EMOTIONAL FALLOUT FROM CHILD IDENTITY THEFT

This section focuses on the emotional toll identity theft can take on the victim and his or her family and offers suggestions for dealing with it.

QUESTION #74: HOW DO I EXPLAIN IDENTITY THEFT TO MY CHILD?

You have taken the first step by picking up this book in an effort to educate yourself on this destructive crime. Your challenge will be to educate yourself and your family on how to successfully survive in a financial world where there are no absolute protections. Key to surviving successfully is accepting the belief that your child's identity is of value and needs protection and theft prevention.

Take what you absorb and translate it into a discussion your children will understand. This means translating the legal terms and phrases that law enforcement uses to describe something into simple verbiage that your child can understand. Don't panic; you are the best there is at communicating with your child. Go slowly, use basic terms, and encourage them to come back to you with questions.

Criminals are targeting children at birth, so you are already at a disadvantage. I recommend that you start young. Do not wait for a specific age, such as when they start school or when they get their first computer. According to a 2008 research project study conducted by Javelin Strategy and Research,[1] 12 percent of all children experiencing child identity theft issues are under the age of five. Start discussions as soon as your children can understand who you are versus a stranger. Child identity theft is not just about finances, it is about a predator targeting your child because of his or her age.

A good child identity theft discussion with children should include the following topics:

- What is personal or private information? Children understand private body parts but may have no concept of what personal information is or that it can be abused. I would cover name, date of birth, and address if the child is very young. If your child is over six years old, I would add phone numbers and phone usage, Social Security numbers, and computer safety to your discussion. Covering the "basics" appropriate for a particular age group is fine, but the conversation is a must. Parents are the best people to decipher what their child can absorb at what age. After your initial discussion, revisiting the topic of child identity theft as they mature is a great idea.

- Parents set the ground rules for their children as they are growing up. Use this influence to set healthy guidelines on who should have access to your child's information. When your child understands this, they will be less intimidated.
- Teach your child to communicate with you, as well as advise you who is asking for their information. Be informed about your child's life by asking them to tell you when someone wants to know their personal information.
- Reinforce not talking to strangers. It is fine to be courteous, it's "gentlemanly" to hold the door for someone, it may sound respectable to hear your child respond to someone with "yes, ma'am" or "yes, sir," but teach your children to resist giving out personal information to strangers.
- Reinforce a child's right to say NO to things that make them uncomfortable. If anyone asks your child something that makes them uncomfortable, he or she should have the right to consult with you before answering. This is not disrespectful but rather protective from many aspects.
- View computers as a launching platform that connects your child with the rest of the world. Discuss the benefits of such technology and the education that can be gained from knowledge. Reinforce the dangers that can be found as well as the benefits. Set parameters on what can and cannot be viewed and discuss why unapproved sites are dangerous. Remember, if you do not have these conversations with your child, someone else will who may not share your opinions.

QUESTION #75: WHAT EMOTIONAL IMPACT WILL CHILD IDENTITY THEFT HAVE ON MY FAMILY?

The emotional trauma a child experiences in child identity theft is real. One of the best descriptions that capture the feelings during this emotionally charged period is the emotional "roller-coaster effect." Prepare yourself and your child mentally to experience an emotional roller coaster of feelings when dealing with child identity theft issues. The emotions may be a result of an event that occurred, a phone call received, an interview conducted, a letter received, or some other type of issue you are dealing with. You will experience "highs" on good days, thinking you are making great progress, and "lows" on days in which you think there is no end.

The first emotion usually experienced by a child identity theft victim and his or her parents or guardians is disbelief. As a family, how could you not have seen it coming? What were the signs that you missed? Who were you in contact with that could have done this to you or your child? How long has this been going on? Why would someone target your child?

Other common emotions experienced are anger, frustration, and feelings of helplessness. Most do not even know the crime exists until they have been victimized. Once victimized, denial is a waste of time for both you and your child. The time spent in denial would be better spent on solving the problem.

Whether your case is an eighteen-year-old who has found out they were victimized as a child, or a parent who has discovered their child has been victimized, the traumatic emotions are the same. There is nothing abnormal about feeling violated by a criminal stealing something as close and personal as your name. Child identity theft is much like many other crimes that affect a person's safety and feelings of change in their ability to be protected, or protect others.

Being victimized leaves you with a feeling of insecurity. From your child's point of view, it may be the first time that you, as the parent or guardian, could not protect them from harm. Your child's perspective on safety may be altered somewhat by the event. Provide your child with comfort and reassurance. Their view of you in action fighting for them will be long lasting and will help them understand that with victimization can be the strong support and love from those they trust the most in their lives.

Another important point to note up front is that this crime is not just a personal crime of finances but rather a crime that is emotionally damaging with a wide path of those it affects. The further along you get into resolving your child's victimization, the more you will agree that it is not your child alone who will be damaged emotionally. Child identity theft is a hurtful crime that will emotionally impact your entire family.

Building a strong support system is essential. My first suggestion is to include those around you who would normally be of help and emotional support during a crisis. Understand that most of the necessary cleanup can only be done by you. Creditors, banks, credit referral agencies, and others burned once by an identity thief will require positive identification when dealing with you on the cleanup. Gather all documents you can find to prove your child does in fact belong to you. Contact law enforcement and request that a report be taken. Use the checklist this book provides to ensure you have taken the necessary steps to clear your child's name.

Family members, if not the perpetrators, are great to assist you with collecting the child's birth certificate, Social Security card, school report cards, school IDs, passports, military IDs (if a military dependent), photos, and other documents to prove the child is who you indicate he or she is. Be prepared to have to prove who you are as well.

QUESTION #76: WHAT EMOTIONAL TRAUMA CAN PARENTS EXPECT TO EXPERIENCE IN CHILD IDENTITY THEFT?

Significant emotional damage is done to a parent as well as the child. The first and worst is definitely guilt. Feeling guilty that you could have done more to protect your child is normal. The best advice I can provide is if you have already been victimized, learn from what has happened and never accept the "it won't happen to me or my child" philosophy. If you haven't been a victim, start protecting your child now by taking proactive steps to protect your child's identity.

If you take proactive steps to ensure your child's safety, there is little cause to feel guilty. Realize that there is no 100 percent guarantee of child protection throughout life. Consider it much like talking to your child about the dangers of drugs, setting a good example, and then hoping they make the right decisions. Not exactly on point, I understand, because what a stranger, friend, or relative does to you or your child may be unpreventable. The point is this, though: did you take steps to secure your child's identity? Did you lock up their birth certificate? Did you talk to them about releasing information about themselves?

You cannot stand over your child twenty-four hours a day. They must go to school, visit relatives, play sports, play with other children, and have a normal life. You want normal interaction so they will be socially healthy. In addition to setting a good example in life, give them the skills they need to be successful, such as teaching them not to release personal information.

To restate my point, once you have taken proactive steps, you have little cause for guilt. If your child is still victimized, then focus your energy on cleaning up the mess and bringing the criminal to justice by assisting law enforcement. Channel your efforts into cleaning up the false items listed on credit reports, closing fraudulent credit card accounts, and notifying providers that your child is not of age to have opened service accounts.

It will not be an easy process. In addition to feeling angry about being violated, be prepared to experience embarrassment during the process of healing and cleaning up the mess. Embarrassment is common when interacting with other parents, school officials, relatives, and people you will deal with to fix the problems. It will go hand in hand with the guilt you will experience when you feel you "let" this happen to your child.

Some of the feelings of embarrassment will come from the belief you may have, in some way, contributed to the theft of your child's identity. Understand that both you and your child are victims. No one asks to be a victim of crime. Victimization requires healing, as trusting again does not come easy. Clear up the problem and then take preventive steps toward reducing the chances of it happening again.

Burnout is real. Be prepared to experience burnout on several levels if your case is not solved quickly. You, first and foremost, will become tired of dealing with creditors, banks, credit reporting agencies, and law enforcement. Even if they are trying to help you, it will still drain you emotionally to share the same information over and over again. Things you might have enjoyed before, like getting the mail out of the mailbox, will become dreaded acts. Opening the box to find another bill, another collection notice, or worse, a court document will invoke feelings of anger.

Be prepared for reduced support as this drags on. It is imperative you solve identity theft as quickly as possible. I understand that this is out of your control most times. Cleaning up the mess as quickly as possible is important because those around you will eventually become numb to your stories, pain, and the events happening to you. Given their initial disbelief and anger, I know it is hard to believe and imagine their support would decline, but it is very true. Others' lives must go on, but yours will be put on hold.

Child identity theft is not always solved quickly. Identities can be stolen, sold, and then resold several times. If you are lucky, it will be stolen once and the thief caught quickly. Your case could involve many jurisdictions and many years of abuse. Determination will be what brings your suffering to an end.

QUESTION #77: I'M THE ONE WHO TOOK MY CHILD'S IDENTITY. WHAT SHOULD I DO?

There are two important aspects of concern when a parent steals from a child. The first is legal, and the second is emotional. Both aspects are high priority, and choosing between them is tough. Parents stealing their children's identities usually do so for one of two reasons.

The first is to provide for the child. In doing so, they justify the theft by saying that they have used the child's identity to provide care that they would not have been able to maintain or obtain otherwise. Providing care, in this example, might come in the form of a utility service, such as a power company connection. It might also be a water hookup or a fuel or oil account for a home heating system. These services are basic care services. Extended basic services might include a credit account for food, or the purchase of a basic vehicle for transportation.

Besides the obvious theft and violation, the problem with "borrowing" your child's identity to obtain services is that it becomes a gateway to abuse. Most parents start the process saying that they will only do it for a short period to get through a tough time. The reality is that once it is done, a crime has been committed.

It is rare that parents stop at basic service needs. This brings us to the second reason parents steal a child's identity, which is greed. As sad as it sounds, the history of child identity theft actually shows that stealing a child's identity for basic services usually leads to using the same continuation of theft for items of luxury, such as electronics, higher-priced vehicles, and credit cards that will never be paid off.

Parents stealing from their children do so in part because they feel they could never be caught, and if they are caught, who would testify against them? Certainly not their child, right? Foster parents and temporary foster parents who commit child identity theft feel like the child stayed with so many sets of parents, possibly in many foster care facilities, that by the time the child turns eighteen years old, he or she will never remember, or be able to prove, who stole their identity.

So where does that leave the child? From an emotional standpoint, it leaves them in need of counseling. If you took your child's identity, you need to fix the damage and seek family counseling so that a professional can assist each family member with the healing process. If you fail to rectify the problem correctly, you may find yourself related to a child that feels bitterness and hatred toward you for the abuse you have caused.

As the bitterness grows, you may also find yourself in civil court. A child does have the right to sue their parents whether they are over the age of eighteen or not. The lawsuit can be for amounts owed while using the stolen name or for punitive damages and emotional harm caused by the theft. While most parents would consider this extreme, it cannot be ruled out, as it is a viable option for the victim.

This brings us to the overall issue of trust. Every child needs the ability to trust someone. Destroyed trust is one of the sad realities of child crimes. Much like child sexual abuse, identity theft cases that involve parents leave children with the fear that those charged with their protection no longer can be trusted. Once you lose the trust of your child, gaining it back may be difficult, if not impossible.

If you find yourself in financial trouble, seek financial advice from your bank or someone you can trust about financial matters. Ask if there are additional hours available to work at your current job, understanding that you may also have to explore an additional job to generate more income. If possible, obtain a loan to get you through a tough period, or ask other family members for help if that is an option. Be creative in resolving your financial situation, as you are ultimately responsible for all debt incurred in your name. Show your children you care by protecting them and providing them with a fair chance at success in adulthood. Avoid child identity theft as a solution to financial problems for your children's sake.

QUESTION #78: HOW SHOULD I HANDLE IT WHEN THE THIEF TURNS OUT TO BE A RELATIVE?

Healing is easier said than done when the thief is a relative. Most children look to relatives as elders, mentors, and protectors. A helpful relative can have a strong relationship in a child's life. The wrong kind of family relationship occurs when a relative is not the helpful kin but rather the harmful foe. Picture this scenario: your child comes of age only to find out that a relative "borrowed" his or her Social Security number somewhere along the way, and now the young adult has a ruined credit history.

This crime is real and occurs every day. It could have been a one-time theft or a repeated purchasing spree for items of fun and luxury. It also could have been to obtain a job or purchase a home. Regardless of the reason, though, it is illegal, unfair, and emotionally abusive to the victim. Child identity theft committed by a relative leaves a child with feelings of betrayal.

According to the U.S. Department of Justice, Office of Justice Programs, "Family identity theft, sometimes called intergenerational identity theft, may be the easiest of these crimes to commit, because the perpetrator has ready access to the victim's personal information. Identity theft among family members is frequently regarded as a personal family matter, not a crime. However, this crime leaves victims feeling as though they had been victimized twice—first by the family member, and then by the system, which will not help them unless a police report is filed. Discord among family members is common in these types of cases."[2]

The challenge for victims and their immediate family members will be finding a way to channel the hurt, aggressive feelings, and anger into productive action. What I am trying to convey is that your available time is critical when cleaning up child identity theft. I encourage you to maximize your efforts toward contacting creditors and credit-reporting agencies and coordinating with law enforcement officials on your case. Extra time should be devoted to your child and his or her mental health.

The question you, as a parent, will have to answer is whether or not you are going to notify the police. If you know from the beginning it was a family member, what will you do? Your thoughts may be that it would only make matters worse. The truth is that you will only make matters worse by not addressing it in the proper way. If not addressed, relatives may feel free to do it again, thinking that you are intimidated and will never call law enforcement.

Child identity theft cases not reported may never get resolved. Some entities will refuse to fix your child identity theft issue unless you report the incident to law enforcement and provide them with a police incident report. If you refuse to have the police investigate the case, and entities refuse to fix the issue, then the one hurt most in this situation is your child. The child will retain all negative information on their credit file and will not be able to make credit purchases as simple as buying furniture on credit, or as complex as buying land or a home.

In most cases of identity theft where a relative is involved, law enforcement will discover the fact that a relative committed the crime through their investigation. You will not know who the thief is until you meet with the law enforcement officer investigating your case to receive an update. At this point, you may or may not be in control of the outcome. You may not want charges to be brought against your relative, or to have your case prosecuted, but it may be law enforcement or the prosecutor who gets to make the final decision in those matters.

Regardless of what stage the investigation is in when you find out a relative committed the crime, you need to move forward just as if it was a stranger. Keep the mindset that your child has been victimized and neither you nor your child should have to justify the legal outcome. Remember, your child is your top priority, and his or her future depends on your ability to clean up the damage.

QUESTION #79: WHEN MIGHT COUNSELING BE A GOOD IDEA?

Child identity theft is rising at an alarming rate. Your child is but one victim among many, but it is easy to feel like you are going through the process alone. Children can feel angry and powerless. Parents can be paralyzed with guilt for not being able to protect their children. Emotions may rage, but at what point will you make the call on whether or not you should seek counseling?

Counseling needs can manifest themselves in many ways. Begin by looking for obvious signs of trouble: behavior changes, such as fear of interaction with people or fear of going to places the child used to love. Look for personality changes, such as periods of depression, anxiety, fear, and crying spells. Note any personal care changes, such as a lack of showering or problems at school. Children can also manifest out-of-control behaviors, such as drug or alcohol use or violence.

While we may feel that children are young and resilient, the truth is that they are subject to developing adult-like challenges, both physically and mentally, and need nurturing. Look for poor self-esteem development, destructive thoughts, and signs that they are dealing with a crisis negatively. Develop a dialogue with your child and let him or her know that you are willing to help them emotionally, as well as guide them down a path to help clear fraudulent activity to the best of your ability.

You might think that most parents avoid counseling because of a lack of funds, lack of insurance, or high costs. The truth is that most parents avoid counseling not because of costs, but because they feel like they know their children best, and they can handle any emotional needs their children might have. While few people know a child like a parent, a parent might not be the one to deal with the issues that develop from child identity theft if the person committing the crime is a parent or a relative.

Healing requires a strong time commitment. Depending upon the child, it may also require special skills in surfacing pain that a child could be suppressing. Bringing something to the surface to be dealt with and discussed is critical, because hurt does not always manifest itself in clearly visible ways. In most cases, it will take a professional counselor to build a relationship with the child before emotional healing can begin. Once the challenges and pain surface, a counselor can begin to help the child deal with the emotional trauma, and create a path toward healing.

Your support in the process will be important for their success. If your child hears you verbally supporting their counseling efforts, he or she will be more likely to be receptive to the counseling methods. On the other hand, if a child identity theft victim hears parents speaking negatively about counseling or voicing their lack of support toward counseling, the child will most likely resist counseling as well.

If you couple counseling efforts with life changes aimed at preventing a reoccurrence of child identity theft, your child will understand your commitment. If you display a positive attitude and show determination toward resolving the damage done, then your child will see, through your efforts, your commitment to help him or her. Your child will also see the high priority you place on them in your life, which will help in rebuilding trust for the future.

Part of being a role model in life is doing the right thing. Doing the right thing, as you well know, may not always be easy. Counseling decisions are hard decisions, but necessary. Parents who decide to allow their children to see counselors after victimization are showing care and concern their child will always remember. So when is counseling a good idea? It is a good, healthy idea anytime your child displays a genuine need for help to manage through life's challenges.

6

PREVENTING CHILD
IDENTITY THEFT

This section discusses ways the government, parents, and educators can help protect children from identity theft.

QUESTION #80: WHAT ARE THE TOP TEN MISTAKES PARENTS MAKE THAT CONTRIBUTE TO CHILD IDENTITY THEFT?

1. Mistake #1 is failing to educate your child and your family on child identity theft. When you fail to educate your family on child identity theft, you are contributing to their victimization. Family members do not automatically recognize the value of a child's identity; therefore, they do not protect it.

2. Mistake #2 is releasing too much information. Parents release, or approve the release, of their child's information too often without questioning what the person, business, or organization will do with the information. One example of this would be online systems, such as Facebook, that ask a new user for his or her name, date of birth, and e-mail information. Are you sure you are comfortable with your child providing a date of birth for this purpose? Is it really necessary?

3. Mistake #3 is not preventing child identity theft at school. Parents seldom band together to influence school systems to protect children's information. School protections are usually limited to student identification numbers and computer firewalls that are really designed to protect the school's computer rather than the student's identity. Parents need to raise the issue of teacher and administration education on child identity theft and cause grassroots changes throughout the school in all grades.

4. Mistake #4 is failing to properly dispose of identifying documents. Most parents throw away documents that could be used as identifying information or intelligence on your children and family. Some people tear paper documents. The best way to destroy a document is with a cross-cutting shredder. If you do not have access to a shredder, you can soak documents in water or burn them.

5. Mistake #5 is failing to take advantage of free services. Parents can receive a free annual benefits and earnings statement from the Social Security Administration. If a thief has used your child's Social Security number to obtain employment, the earnings will show up on this document. Parents and children can request a free annual credit

report. Parents can place a free ninety-day credit alert on their child's credit report if they feel they need to for additional protection.

6. Mistake #6 is carrying too much information about your child in your wallet or purse. If it is lost or stolen, what would a stranger find out about your child?

7. Mistake #7 is establishing a work space that says too much about your children. Parents love their children and want to display their accomplishments; however, knowledge is intelligence to a child identity thief. Your information can be compromised by a coworker, janitorial after-hours employee, or a service provider with access to your office.

8. Mistake #8 is computer breaches. Parents fail to establish virus protection, firewalls, and strong passwords.

9. Mistake #9 is failing to monitor social networking and gaming site usage. Children and young adults give out an enormous amount of unsafe information about themselves and their family. For example, the advanced systems in Xbox 360 can be fun, as they will allow the user to play with other players not present in your home. If you or your child wants to register to enjoy this form of entertainment, Xbox wants you to provide your date of birth. To whom is your child providing his or her date of birth? Is this safe? You be the judge.

10. Mistake #10 is failing to verify medical data when visiting a hospital or doctor. If your child was victimized by an identity thief and that information was used for medical care, then a free credit report is not going to help. Review your insurance statements very carefully, and verify hospital and doctor records periodically to ensure your child is the only one using his or her identity.

QUESTION #81: IS THE GOVERNMENT DOING ANYTHING TO COMBAT IDENTITY THEFT?

By now you have read a lot of information about how harmful child identity theft is, how widespread the effects are, and the preventive measures you can take to help your child. This brings us to the question of what our government is doing to assist us in combating this new-age crime. Are agencies and systems dedicating resources to fighting the crime of child identity theft?

The short answer is yes. There appears to be a broad or generic-approach effort under way that lacks the lightning-bolt effect of citizen involvement. The federal government has designated a lead agency for gathering statistics. This agency, the Federal Trade Commission (FTC), is a good resource for information and reporting.

The FTC website has great resources. This site, located at www.ftc.gov, is for citizens, law enforcement, businesses, military, and media. It is also a reference for state and national statistics on the crime of identity theft. The starting point for most people is viewing the site to file a complaint after victimization. I encourage you to explore the site as a preventive measure and take advantage of the great information that will help protect you and your family.

The FTC's motto is "Deter, Detect, and Defend," and they have designed their assistance around these three areas. *Deter* is all about prevention at FTC. *Prevention* means minimizing your risk and exposure. Risk and exposure are addressed through protecting your Social Security number and understanding the importance of shredding documents. It is also about what you put in the garbage, how to safeguard your valuables, and dealing with the Internet and computers.

Detecting identity theft involves knowing the signs to look for, how to verify that your identity has been stolen, and how to take advantage of the annual free credit report. The *defend* aspect of the FTC's effort deals with recovering from the crime after finding out you have become a victim. The FTC provides you with information on fraud alerts and credit freezes. They also provide a guide to reporting the crime to law enforcement, and help you with tips on what to do during the reporting process.

The FTC's site also assists businesses. Browse the site for information on how a business can help citizens who have been victimized, how to deal with data breaches, and how to safeguard your information. For law enforcement agencies, the FTC site is a reference for laws, publications, and education. Military members can view the site to get information on active duty alerts, tools, and military resources. Finally, the media can view the site for statistical data, press releases, and writing about identity theft.

Another great site for citizens is the U.S. Postal Inspection Service website. This site can be found at https://postalinspectors.uspis.gov/, and also has a wealth of tips, great videos, and informative brochures. View the site and select "Investigations." Once there, click on "Identity Theft," where you will get access to the latest identity theft information, online news, and facts on how thieves steal your name and your money. This website also provides you with the ability to report postal-related identity theft crimes online.

The Social Security Administration attempts to help combat identity theft with the Death Master File. The purpose of this file is to capture death information to prevent criminals from stealing the information of deceased persons for continued use. Unfortunately, the system relies on a variety of sources to report deaths, and it is only partially successful or accurate.

QUESTION #82: WHAT TWO PREVENTIVE MEASURES CAN I TAKE AS A PARENT TO PROTECT MY CHILD FROM IDENTITY THEFT?

The first measure you should take is educating yourself on "opting out." Your child will be targeted for marketing. If they obtain a bank savings account, subscribe to a magazine, join a club, or subscribe to a service, they become potential marketing targets. Many services provided to families include "fine print" marketing. This marketing type usually comes with small print, buried in exhausting instructions, stating that unless you notify the organization that you do not desire to participate in further promotions, programs, or the sharing of your information, they will automatically enroll you. If you neglect to "opt out," your child's identity information may be shared or sold to other businesses or organizations. Opting out for both parents and children is smart and safe.

It is your right as a consumer to prevent the sharing of your information with any third party and any marketing group, mailing list, survey group, e-mail address collector, or collector of information that is shared. How does this help your child? It helps in two ways: first, it cuts down on solicitation phone calls coming into the house and junk mail delivered to your mailbox.

Second, you have better control over who markets to your children, and which companies share or sell your child's identity. Beyond the desire to cut down on mail and phone calls, "opting out" reduces the access thieves have to your family's personal information, thereby reducing the chance your child's identity would be compromised. Some organizations resell client information for profit. "Opting out" can help prevent additional holders of your child's identity from sharing or selling confidential information. Some businesses do not share or sell your information but are hacked by computer thieves who use their knowledge to get inside a computer system and steal personal identity information. Hackers break into business computer systems every day, stealing customer data. This concern alone should warrant a strong consideration to "opt out" with any company that does not need identity information from you or your child stored in their database system.

I recommend that you protect yourself with a full-scale "opt out" of any entity with which you do business. Reducing incoming mail and phone calls allows you to manage and provide oversight on incoming mail and calls that come in. It is much easier to review mail each day if you reduce the "junk" coming into your household. This same concept allows you to take just a moment, with this reduced-mail effort, to see who is sending your child offers, advertisements, and magazines. It also helps you with nuisance phone calls and reduces the amount of time you will have to take reviewing the caller ID.

When you begin your quest to opt out, your first contact should be to the FTC at (888) 5-OPTOUT (888-567-8688). This phone line is managed by the Federal Trade Commission to assist individuals in the opt-out process. Select your desire to opt out and the FTC converts your request into a notice advising potential businesses that they are prohibited under law to market, sell, or use your information. This is the best call you can make, since it affects all four of the credit reporting agencies and is good for five years. It is a telephone system that is easy to navigate and short in duration.

You can also opt out via the Internet. If you have Internet access, just type in www.optoutprescreen.com in your web browser, then hit the "enter" button on your keyboard. Once there, you have three different options. Option one is "opting in"; disregard this unless you want to be included on lists that are used to offer credit and insurance. Option two is opting out electronically for five years. This option excludes you from having to receive offers for five years. Option three is permanently opting out. To complete this option, you must print the form provided on the website and mail it to the address provided.

"Opting in" or "opting out" via the telephone system or the Internet is a one-source task. In other words, you do not have to make a call or visit a site for different credit reporting agencies, opting out of each. Just visit the site I have provided, and one call or one click handles your desires with all credit reporting agencies.

If you are opting out of mail offers to reduce the amount of "junk" mail and your potential exposure to identity theft, I recommend you also register with the Do Not Call Registry. This will cut down on the number of un-wanted telemarketer calls seeking information and asking you to purchase goods and services. To begin this process, call (888) 382-1222, or go to their website, which is www.donotcall.gov.

If you visit the Do Not Call Registry website, it will tell you that phone numbers remain permanently once placed and do not need reentering peri-odically. Just begin by following the instructions under the tab "Registering a Phone Number." You will enter the data and provide an e-mail address for verification purposes. Once you receive the e-mail and verify it, you will be permanently listed. I recommend this to protect your children from answering the phone and giving out information you would not condone. In addition to children, this is also a good idea for the elderly. Make sure to include all phone numbers that each family member has established in his or her name.

QUESTION #83: IF I AM A TEACHER, WHAT CAN I DO TO PROTECT MY STUDENTS?

Teachers make a difference in children's lives every day. They are viewed as educators, mentors, and guardians. Teachers have the ability to reach chil-dren in critical ways. As educators, teachers can help young students learn what child identity theft is and why prevention is important.

As mentors, teachers can set a good example and be proactive in pre-venting child identity theft, thus showing they care. As guardians, teachers take on the role of protectors. Influence the education system from within, encouraging financial education beyond personal finances. Help school administrators understand the necessity for classroom time on the topic of child identity theft and its harmful effects.

Teachers influence children each and every day. This is why they are a great starting point for education on child identity theft. Before starting, though, let's take a moment to ensure you are using the prevention tips this book offers for your profession. Listed below are suggested items that you can do, or participate in, that will help your school take a more proactive approach in the protection of your students.

Teacher/School Tips

- Have you removed any wall charts announcing student names and dates of birth?
- Do you keep all room file cabinets containing student information locked when you are out of the room?
- Do you lock your desk at night and anytime you are out of the classroom?
- If you maintain a grade book, have you replaced student names with school-issued student ID numbers?
- Do you shred all documents when discarding them instead of throwing them in the trash?
- If your school maintains student information on computer systems, do you have password policies and download policies and require that the computers request a password when left unattended for any length of time?
- Do you provide your students with any education on what child identity theft is?
- Have you discussed child identity theft with your school administration?
- Does your school system do background checks on all employees in every role?
- Does your school limit the sharing of student information to those who need to know, such as the child's actual teacher and not just a school system employee?

- Have you discussed the topic of child identity theft with parent-teacher association (PTA) leaders at your school, and with parents at a PTA meeting or other forum?
- Have you contacted your state police, local police, or sheriff's office to see if they have an officer who can come to your school and speak on child identity theft?
- Does your school encourage reporting suspicious acts?
- Does your school have a visitor badge system?

As a teacher, you are recognized as a select respected group within society that develops and cares for children not their own. Teachers can best make a difference with this new crime by being a catalyst for education and change. Child identity theft steals a child's chance for a fresh start as an adult; thus, education of parents, school system employees, and students are a must if we are to defeat this crime. While parents can influence the child and the system from outside, teachers can influence both from within.

QUESTION #84: MY CHILD IS IN DAY CARE. WHAT PRECAUTIONS SHOULD I TAKE TO PROTECT THEIR IDENTITY?

Protecting your child begins with the selection of your day care facility. Your selection process begins with a list of the items you desire in care. Most parents seek a day care that is certified by the state as approved. This approval usually means that they understand the state's mandates for care. Many states regulate and license child day care centers. In addition to the licensing process, state licensing representatives visit and inspect conditions for compliance.

State licensing representatives may look at the functional design of the business location, the ratio of care providers to children, the presence of asbestos, and the presence of proper fire extinguishing equipment. They may require a criminal background check of all employees. They will probably set high standards for good hygiene. Your state will most likely govern and regulate many other items, but one area they will likely fall short in is identification security and identity theft.

Your choice of location should include a center that will protect your child's information. Look at the forms they require. What personal data are they asking for? Once they receive it, how are they set up to secure it? When finished with the document, what do they do with it? Do they have a shredder? If they have computers, are they entering your child's information in them? If so, do they password-protect the computers?

When you search for your desired child day care center, you should be considering the safety of your child, and in doing so, visually inspect the security. Good security starts on the outside of the building with video cameras, fencing, and play areas that are safely away from the road. It continues to the inside with secure files and locked drawers to protect children's personal information. It also includes computers with hard passwords and computer monitors out of the view of the public.

Inquire how employees are screened. Ask if all employees are screened with background checks or just employees who directly care for the children. Remember that clerical, administrative, and janitorial staff play a role in child identity theft due to their access to information. Ask who will have access to your child's information, both during and after hours. Ask if there is a system at the care facility where the children wear identification bracelets, necklaces, or tags during the care hours for tracking should a child get lost or taken.

Most day care providers do a good job of focusing on the physical care of their children. However, they most likely do not understand child identity theft and how their actions and facility figure into the equation. Do not be surprised if you, as the parent or guardian, are more educated on the topic of child identity theft than the day care provider. This is a good opportunity to team your provider up with a law enforcement crime prevention specialist. A crime prevention specialist can help the day care facility staff understand the aspects and elements of child identity theft, and the positive changes that their day care environment can make to prevent a theft occurrence at their location.

Should you decide to leave the day care and switch to another, it is important that you retrieve any remaining paperwork they have on your child. Once your child permanently leaves the day care facility, they will have less reason to secure the information. Ask the provider for a letter stating that they have permanently deleted any and all information on your child from their computer systems. You will want to ask for any individual records a teacher, supervisor, or employee may have been keeping on your child. Lastly, ask them if your child may have left behind any remaining property to include clothes, backpacks, or lunch boxes. These are important steps that must be taken by you as the protector of your child's identification information.

QUESTION #85: WHAT IS "CRAMMING," AND WHAT CAN I DO ABOUT IT?

Cramming is a scam, and it can happen to both children and adults. Cramming happens when an organization bills its customer, adding charges that the customer did not authorize or agree to. If your child orders a magazine subscription, automated delivery of a product, a monthly service, or any item for which they are billed, they could get scammed through cramming if you are not diligent in viewing the bill each time it comes in.

Cramming affects young adults more often than small children because young adults are more involved in purchasing, ordering, and subscribing to services that require billing. Cramming is increasingly difficult to uncover, since many bills are directly sent to teenagers through e-mail. Most businesses try to get customers to agree to a paperless delivery of their bill in order to reduce billing costs. While this is a savings to the business, it does little to help parents.

Parents need to insist that when bills are sent to their children, the parent also receives a copy. Parents should be familiar with the service and the agreed-upon terms from the start. Each bill received should be cautiously reviewed for items within the bill. Added fees, purchases, and items not originally agreed upon need to be questioned. Dispute any item that you or your child did not approve before delivery. Cancel any service that dishonestly added an item, even if they claim it was a mistake.

Cramming can happen in any bill. Some bills are easy to review, and some are not. An example is a phone bill. Deciphering the federal fees, state taxes, and local charges can be complex. Businesses who cram take advantage of this fact and add not-agreed-upon costs to your bill. Your best weapon is your ability to call and dispute, or cancel, the service.

As with your phone bill, a very important point to make is that cramming does not always involve large fees or big-purchase items. Remember, small items add up when you bill a multitude of people successfully. Many businesses have thousands of customers. If each customer is billed a small fee of fifty cents or one dollar without question, then the business has the opportunity to make hundreds or thousands of dollars. If only a few people question the fee, then the multitude make the fraud worth the cramming. Once the cramming charge remains on the bill without question, it becomes legitimate in the mind of the consumer, who is even less likely to question it than before.

Parents who find cramming charges should take action. Cramming should be reported to the Better Business Bureau. Reporting puts both the business and other potential consumers on notice that the business has questionable practices. A negative rating with the Better Business Bureau alerts consumers that a business is potentially a bad investment of both time and money, and should be avoided.

How can you help reduce cramming incidents? Deal only with reputable businesses. Avoid enter-to-win sweepstakes that request your personal information. Avoid "join the club" services that indicate all you have to do is provide your name and authorization for the service. Things too good to be true usually are. Avoid "free" calls that start with 1-900 (***-****). 900 numbers are not free; they are charging you by the minute for your call.

A good resource for cramming is the Federal Trade Commission's Consumer Sentinel Network. This network can be viewed on the web at http://www.ftc.gov/sentinel/. The Consumer Sentinel is a resource for consumer tips, statistics, and data collection. Check it out; it is worth the time.

QUESTION #86: HOW CAN I KEEP UP WITH EVER-EVOLVING SCAMS?

If you look at scams conducted across the nation, you will see that the most common trait among them is not the age, race, geographical area, or financial status of the potential victim, but rather the scammers' desire to make quick and easy money. Scams do target specific groups of individuals, such as children, but they do it for monetary reasons. Thieves see vulnerability and seize the opportunity. This is very common not only with children, but also elderly adults.

The ultimate goal of a scam is to get you to part with your money. It is not that you will not question the transaction, but you will ultimately carry through with it. Seldom do thieves come back to the person scammed unless the case is child identity theft. In child identity theft, thieves repeatedly victimize the child because the child is completely unaware the crime has been committed.

Just as quickly as you catch on to scams, others seem to evolve. This is a daily challenge for law enforcement. Before you can completely understand a crime and evolutions of the initial crime, thieves are on to the next new crime. Child identity theft is just such a crime. What starts with identity theft becomes a bonanza when the thieves discover they can target children instead of adults and increase their profit hundreds of times over with repeated use. This is the number-one reason that children are fifty-one times more likely to be targeted than adults.

Fortunately, law enforcement has many tools available to assist parents and guardians with fraud cleanup. Citizens also have ways they can educate themselves on trending crimes and how to report them. One of the tools available to consumers is the Consumer Sentinel Network. The Consumer Sentinel Network provides information on identity theft, Do Not Call violations, telemarketing, computer crimes, sweepstakes, lotteries, prize scams, work-from-home scams, weight loss scams, and loan scams.

The Federal Bureau of Investigation (FBI) offers excellent resources for citizens seeking information on scams. These educational resources can be viewed through their website and include education on how to protect your children from crimes. You may research this information on the FBI website at www.fbi.gov.

A visit to the site can offer you information on the latest scam trending. The website also offers information on a wide range of scams, including jury duty scams, financial scams, common fraud scams, dating scams, and tips for potential senior victims. Looking to protect your child? This site gives you information on club drugs, crimes against children, missing and exploited children, gangs, and gun safety.

You can help the FBI prevent terrorism and terrorist attacks, thereby increasing the safety of your children. Have you observed something lately that appeared out-of-the-ordinary, such as someone taking photographs, making maps, recording activities, or conducting surveillance outside of a government building, military facility, or a local or national landmark?

If you ever witness suspicious activities, report them. The information you share may be just what the FBI needs to uncover a threat, or solve a crime. Your commitment to share information regarding illegal activity will help law enforcement reduce crime in your community.

Other great scam resources include the Federal Trade Commission, www.ftc.gov, and the U.S. Postal Inspection Service, https://postal inspectors.uspis.gov/. Scams are committed by unscrupulous individuals. While keeping up with scams can be challenging, it comes down to determination. Scams can be defeated with a concerted effort by law enforcement, the media, and citizen involvement.

QUESTION #87: HOW DO I MAKE SURE I'M NOT CARRYING THINGS IN MY WALLET THAT COULD OPEN MY CHILD UP TO IDENTITY THEFT?

In the late 1600s, a pocket-sized tool was invented to store cash and other small articles of value. This invention was timely, as a paper-style currency followed in the late 1690s. Prior to the wallet, the common item used to carry money was a drawstring-type bag, as the available currency was coinage. Now we fast-forward to the twentieth century and the development of the billfold-type wallet for cash and credit cards, an identity thief's best friend.

At some point in a young boy's life, he will receive his first wallet. At or about the same time, if not before, a young girl will receive her first purse. Mom and dad will encourage them to put his or her name and address in the item to identify its owner, because they feel it certainly will be lost, misplaced, or forgotten. Thus, the ritual of carrying a wallet or purse with identity information begins. For those who have never suffered the misplacement, loss, or theft of such a device, read on. For those who have, I am confident you can relate to what I am about to explain.

During the past four years, at least three different news organizations have written articles on a Salt Lake City man who has been victimized by identity theft for over seventeen years.[1,2] His predator was a German immigrant who, in 2007, was charged with eighty-one counts of identity theft. The ordeal began back in 1985 when he lost his wallet. The lost wallet contained his birth certificate, driver's license, and Social Security card. The first crime committed using the victim's identity was driving under the influence. This was followed by vandalism, burglary, leaving the scene of an accident, making a bomb threat, and more.

Identity theft can happen to individuals of all ages. It can happen to the child who leaves a purse or wallet behind because they do not understand the value of his or her name and date of birth. It can happen to the elderly woman who cannot remember where she left her purse, or the middle-aged businessman who is so busy he leaves even his car keys in places he cannot remember.

What you carry in your wallet does say a lot about you. It can tell an objective party, such as a thief, where you live, who you are, when you were born, and what your Social Security number is. It can also tell a thief who your creditors are. Thieves get some idea of whether or not you have income when they see the number of credit card companies willing to give you credit.

Whether you are a parent, guardian, or family member of a child, chances are that you carry a wallet or purse with photos and information about your children close to you. In most cases, if you carry your child's Social Security card, or name and date of birth written on a piece of paper, you are not alone. Carrying your child's information in your purse or wallet increases the risk that your child will be victimized.

Most parents who lose a purse or wallet, whether it is momentarily or for a longer period of time, are thrilled when it is returned. The returned item is usually visually inventoried quickly for money and then forgotten. The danger of lost or misplaced articles is that a child identity thief takes nothing, but records everything. Let me reiterate that. A child identity thief takes nothing, but records everything.

Child identity thieves do not want to raise your suspicion and cause alarm. They want to successfully use your child's identity for long periods of time. This is why you might get your article of value back without missing cash, credit cards, or other items that may give the appearance of theft. My recommendation is that you go back through the items in your purse or wallet and look for anything out of place.

You should carefully review your wallet or purse for any suspicious activity. Is your driver's license put back the way you usually carry it? Are all the photos placed the correct way? Are the photos in the order in which you normally carry them? Is any portion of your photo holder torn where someone may have had trouble getting an old photo out? If you carry a purse, have the items been moved from one compartment to another? If you carry a wallet, can you tell if someone has been through your items even though you have all the cash?

Parents need to continuously think "child identity theft." Whereas, in the past, the most you might have done in the case of a theft was to cancel your credit cards, now you have to go one or two steps further. If you lose an item that carries valuables, you need to place a ninety-day credit alert on your credit file, as well as on the credit file of each of your children. After the ninety-day alert, request a free credit report to ensure both you and your children were not victimized.

QUESTION #88: HOW CAN A PAPER SHREDDER PROTECT MY CHILD?

One of the best home and office security devices is not an alarm, but rather a paper-shredding device. This is essential for properly destroying documents with personal information. Most individuals will tear paper documents before throwing them in the trash. Have childhood games and puzzles not taught us for many years that things taken apart can be reassembled to reveal a picture? If a child can re-create a puzzle, surely an adult can piece together torn-up identification information. The difference: an adult is not playing a game.

When contemplating whether to shred your paperwork or not, look at the definition of trash. Trash is something discarded or no longer desired or wanted. This is not only a layman's version, but a legal interpretation by courts as well. It opens your trash up to being rifled through by whoever has access to it once it leaves your possession. It is what the court refers to when they say that you no longer have an "expectation of privacy" involving what you have thrown away.

It is not uncommon for individuals who live in rural areas to dispose of their garbage in large roadside dumpsters. Even more common is the sight of someone going through those garbage dumpsters seeking that one great find they just can't believe someone threw away. It happens every day, in every rural community in the world.

Identity theft operates in the same manner. You discard your trash, and someone picks it up. Garbage rifling or dumpster diving is common for identity thieves. Thieves use this method because they are successful with it. Those who live in rural areas are not the only victims: trash is trash. Most people who live in urban areas have no idea where their garbage goes once they dispose of it; they just want to get rid of it. Regardless of your system of trash disposal, all trash is susceptible to identity thieves.

To prevent your family from becoming a victim, buy a paper shredder. Most shredding devices are long cut, or vertical. I recommend you go one step further and buy a cross-cutting paper shredder. This cuts paper items into confetti-like, small pieces of paper. Smaller pieces are much more difficult to put back together.

To better protect your family, the following items should be destroyed by a paper shredder versus disposing of the items in the trash:

- Insurance papers no longer needed, desired, and required
- Child birth certificate copies
- Old elementary, middle, or high school information that contains identifiers such as birth date, Social Security number, or address
- Old school transcript copies
- Old child library cards
- Old photo identification cards
- Old mail in your child's name
- Any unnecessary legal documents, such as old court orders
- Old medical records
- Old X-rays that are no longer needed

- School report cards from previous years that you plan to discard
- Old tax returns you no longer need or are required to maintain
- Bank account information in your child's name you plan to discard
- Any investment paperwork that does not need to be retained
- Advertisements your child receives
- Letters your child receives after they have served their purpose

Paper shredders are relatively inexpensive compared to the cost of losing your child's identity. Be proactive in protecting your child's identity by destroying all discarded items in a proper manner. Shredding is a great way to protect your family.

QUESTION #89: WHERE IS THE BEST PLACE TO KEEP OFFICIAL DOCUMENTS RELATING TO MY CHILDREN?

Have you ever had to prove who you were to someone you did not know? It was probably simple because you either had the "proof" required or, in the case of your child, they did not require proof because of their age. Two things have changed as a result of the devastating events of September 11, 2001. The first is that more people and agencies are requiring proof of identity. The second is that required types of proof for identification purposes is strengthening.

When you couple the two facts above with the surge in identity theft to the tune of approximately nine million victims each year, victims find themselves losing the battle when you don't have identifying documents. The end result is that it has become more and more difficult to have someone "accept your word" for identification purposes. Proof of identification might be a driver's license, birth certificate, student identification, bank statement, or passport. Your requirements to obtain these documents are usually a combination of different forms of identification along with a signature, and in some cases, a witness. No need to worry about not having identifying documents, though. The paperwork identifying us begins before we are born with prenatal doctor and hospital visits paving the way for our birth.

Once a child is born, the birth certificate starts the accumulation of mountains of documents we personally need to keep up with throughout our lifetime. So given this, as well as the fact that we are a society of paperwork, how do we do it? How do we safeguard the endless amounts of paperwork and documents we receive and, in particular, how do we safely protect our children's identification documentation?

For some people, documents find their way into a dresser drawer. Others put their documents in a home office or closet. Where is the best place in your home to store documents? Is it in an office, a bedroom, or a closet? Is it under a bed or on top of a shelf? Is it best kept locked or unlocked, and quickly accessible?

The layout of every home is different, and the personal preferences of each homeowner will vary. What is consistent is that each child in your home has personal information that needs some type of protection. The best security is the most stringent. Not everyone, though, can afford the monthly cost of a bank safety deposit box.

I recommend the following commonsense approach. Buy a fireproof document container that provides a locking-type security system. Purchase one that is large enough to hold the family documents you need, or purchase more than one of the same type. These containers should be placed somewhere in the home where parents or guardians can access them, but they are not out in the open; you should be able to get to them without too much trouble.

I am frequently asked about the policy of copying documents and giving these copies to a close family member in case the original is destroyed, stolen, or lost. The possibility of child identity theft by a relative always exists, so you should be cautious to release personal identification records to even family members. If you feel you need to secure a copy of identification records with a trusted relative, you should still monitor your child's credit history by obtaining a credit report yearly.

If you select a locked, fireproof container and a good place in the home to secure it, what documents should you put inside for protection? I recommend the following:

- Birth certificates
- Passports

- Insurance papers
- Marriage certificates
- School diplomas
- Account passwords
- Military discharge papers
- Sensitive medical records
- Automobile titles
- Wills
- Property deeds
- Safe deposit box keys
- Home inventories
- Banking information
- Video of the inside of your home for insurance purposes
- In the case of your death, a list of any person who maintains the possession of any item for safekeeping in another location, and how they can be contacted

Documents relating to your children require the proper safe care. The choice of how you do it is ultimately up to you. The higher level of security you provide for your family's documents, the better chance they have of not being lost, stolen, or destroyed, and thus available for your continued use when needed. Good luck.

QUESTION #90: HOW CAN I PROTECT MYSELF AND MY CHILD WHEN USING SEARCH ENGINES AND WEBSITES?

There are many search engines, but not all are age appropriate. Age-appropriate search engines and websites are those designed specifically for children and young adults. These sites provide information according to the appropriate age category. Listed below are websites that are appropriate for children of different ages. In addition to the sites listed, good resources for children can be found by contacting your child's school library and the public library in your community.

Elementary School Age

- www.kidspace.org
- www.askkids.com
- www.yahooligans.com
- www.ivyjoy.com
- www.kidrex.org
- www.kidsclick.org (School of Library and Information Science at Kent State University)
- www.pctattletale.com
- www.brainpopjr.com
- www.ipl.org (Internet Public Library)
- www.kidskonnect.com
- www.kids.yahoo.com

Middle School/Junior High School Age

- www.askkids.com
- www.awesomelibrary.org
- www.brainpop.com
- www.ipl.org (Internet Public Library)
- www.kidsclick.org (School of Library and Information Science at Kent State University)
- www.kidskonnect.com
- www.kids.yahoo.com
- www.eia.gov/kids/index.cfm (U.S. Energy Information Administration)
- www.gennasworld.com
- www.education.com
- www.whattablast.com

High School Age

- www.awesomelibrary.org
- www.bbc.co.uk/learning
- www.ipl.org (Internet Public Library)

- www.kidsclick.org (School of Library and Information Science at Kent State University)
- www.eia.gov/kids/index.cfm (U.S. Energy Information Administration)
- www.education.com

You control your family policies on web usage and sites visited. In addition to discussing appropriate computer usage with your children and young adults, you can take certain proactive security measures for computers in the home. These measures include establishing blocks for inappropriate websites and controlling your privacy settings to block unsafe pop-ups.

QUESTION #91: WHAT CAN SCHOOLS DO TO HELP SAFEGUARD STUDENTS FROM CHILD IDENTITY THEFT?

An important step in protecting children is to provide education on child identity theft, its aspects, and the harmful effects of not implementing steps to prevent victimization. What seems to be a complex topic is anything but that when you teach age-appropriate aspects of the crime. Child identity theft awareness can be taught by schools and reinforced by parents, or vice versa.

Parents understand the influence that mandatory standardized testing, such as Standards of Learning–type tests, has on school curriculums. Child identity theft is like any other social topic that competes for space with mandated educational topics. The ability to get on the school's curriculum may entirely depend on the prioritization the school administration gives the issue. Schools will be best positioned to help if they have community support or outcry.

The topic of child identity theft is not one that you can just insert into an educational curriculum at a certain grade level. While it is imperative to ensure children are mature enough to grasp the concept of what is being taught, child identity theft education should be continuous. This mindset would allow administrators to begin teaching the dangers of child identity theft to our children at age-appropriate levels throughout their adolescent years. This approach would reinforce the impact of being victimized. Otherwise, children will not have the benefit of the tools necessary to protect themselves from identity theft, making them easier targets.

A better approach is a total partnership between parents and teachers. Parents who are committed to protecting their children begin to emphasize what personal information is, and with whom they are allowed to share it. The best situation to work with is when a schoolteacher of a younger grade level, such as kindergarten or first grade, has a group of children who have a concept of their name, age, and birthday. If allowed within the school system, the teacher could help educate the children on the importance of protecting their name, address, and birthday, as an example, from other classmates, just as they would protect their schoolwork in a protected folder, area, or cubicle. A teacher could use many analogies to help children understand at an earlier age the importance of respecting personal space, and the security of their personal information. This type of coordinated effort between the home and the school administration will help bring more attention to the matters of child identity theft.

As a child mentally develops during the elementary school years, they develop a better concept of personal information and grow in their ability to grasp additional information about themselves. Additional information learned will probably be simple things, such as their telephone number and address. As the child progresses into middle or junior high school, the need progresses for more complex information, such as their Social Security number. Children will begin using computers with, and without, their parents or guardians, operating with a little more freedom.

High school brings the desire to be more independent. Making decisions outside the home away from parents is a very normal transition. This is the age for more complex computer security discussions on topics such as "hard" passwords, security settings, pop-ups, and scams. This is also the appropriate age for an education on finances. Some school systems do teach topics such as checkbook management for young adults. In some educational jurisdictions, a personal finance course is required for a child to graduate from high school. In such a course, it is imperative that our children are taught not only how to open a bank account, balance a checkbook, and pay bills on time, but to protect themselves against identity theft.

The financial crimes in society today mandate a better knowledge of financial issues for children at all ages. Along with the teaching of basic math and checkbook management must be a reinforcement and furtherance of education on child identity theft. This could be a joint project taught with computer and mathematics instructors to enhance all aspects of the mechanisms identity thieves use to get information.

You can help your children. Make it a priority to discuss the topic of a high school financial management course, which includes identity theft, with both your school administration and your school board leaders. Identity theft is a topic that we need to learn at all levels of primary education and retain for the rest of our lives.

QUESTION #92: HOW MIGHT AGE VERIFICATION OF SOCIAL SECURITY NUMBERS HELP PREVENT CHILD IDENTITY THEFT?

If your ten-year-old tried to get a credit card right now, his application may or may not be denied. Theoretically we would like to believe it would be denied because he is too young to enter into a contract. However, if a thief steals your child's Social Security number and applies for a card under your child's name changing the year of birth, there is currently no way to know that something is amiss. The reason is the credit-issuing agencies lack a system of age verification, and for this reason, child identity theft flourishes.

A child identity thief does not have to have all of your child's data. The thief may use a portion of your identity only, as described in "synthetic" identity theft. In either case, the result will probably be the same, issuance of credit using all or a portion of your child's information. Using any of your child's information causes your loved one to accumulate a bad credit record. Bad credit brings the potential for debt collectors and courts to take action against your child and you, as the parent or guardian.

Lack of age-verification capability is a constant factor among all credit-issuing agencies. These agencies recommend credit when queried by credit card companies, lenders, businesses, and more. The systems thrive on "first information submitted." This means that when they have no record of your child, they accept the first submission as the truth, even though an identity thief may have submitted it.

The combination of nonexistent age verification, lack of a birth record system tied into credit issuance, and a Death Master File system without the ability to capture all deaths spells disaster for identity theft victims. These factors allow a child identity thief to scour the newspapers for an infant who has died, because the hospital will be sure to record the birth, but the Death Master File might not capture the death. The same scenario exists for child identity thieves who comb graveyards looking for information.

When a thief obtains your child's information first, they can submit for the Social Security number. This is true whether the child dies and a thief gets his or her information, or whether the thief just gets the information to the Social Security Administration before you do. The end result is that the thief will get the Social Security number and immediately begin to apply for credit in your child's name or number.

So what can parents do to assist their children or protect them where systems do not exist to verify age? Parents can help by understanding child identity theft and put into action the information in this book that provides children with the best protection possible. The first safe practice is to obtain a child's birth certificate at the hospital, and to do so at the earliest opportunity. It should be one of many questions expecting parents ask their hospital staff. As your hospital care team, what is the procedure for obtaining a state birth record or certificate upon birth? Resist the option to obtain the birth certificate at a later date. Any lapse in time is an opportunity for a child identity thief. Next, in planning your trip to the hospital, expecting parents should either visit the Social Security Administration office, or go to their website at www.ssa.gov, and have the Form SS-5 ready for completion and submission as soon as possible.

If you are adopting a child, you need to know if the child has a Social Security number already. If he or she does not, then you might want to wait until you change the child's last name, if that is your plan. In either case, parents seeking to adopt children should take advantage of the annual free credit report and view their child's credit report to see if they have been victimized. Remember the problems foster children face with repeated credit abuse? Do not fall victim to those statistics; follow the steps recommended here, and help guide adopted children on a path to success.

Age verification can stop a large portion of child identity theft. The lack of an age verification system is why children are fifty-one times more likely to be successfully victimized with this financial crime. Until a nation or country can get to the point where it has a system in place, parents shoulder the burden of putting into action their own personal protection plan, and "best practice." Use the information in this book to help you.

QUESTION #93: WHAT ARE MODELING SCAMS, AND HOW CAN THEY AFFECT MY CHILD'S IDENTITY?

Child identity theft prevention comes in many forms. Scams are a tool often used by thieves, so information on types of scams will help you as a parent. One popular scam deals with modeling offers. Modeling scams can affect children of all ages and their parents. Legitimate modeling agencies hire children every day to be in television ads, magazine ads, and newspaper ads.

Children are selected by agencies to represent clothing brands, food items, tourist attractions, and more. Modeling as an industry is legitimate and lucrative, but unregulated. Since modeling does not require government oversight, anyone can be a model, or open an agency. Thieves who use scams as their tool understand a child's desire to be rich, famous, and popular. They know the things to say to children, and the promises to make.

Scammers often use the computer and Internet as their contact method. These allow for anonymous contact from great distances. Foreign countries, such as Nigeria, are infamous for initiating scams. For years, scams, such as the "Nigerian Scam" and the "419 Scam," have plagued the United States, and countries around the world, bilking millions of dollars out of unsuspecting citizens. Foreign scammers use modeling as just one type of scam; they can send their bait in phishing e-mails to children, hoping they will reply.

A modeling scam e-mail baits the child into sending in a photo for evaluation. The return response will be a glowing evaluation of potential. This will be accompanied by fictitious accomplishments the scammer has achieved for other clients the same age, or close to the same age. They may even claim that they have represented stars the children may know from television shows or say that they got the "child star" his or her start in the business. Scammers can say anything, as they know there is virtually no way for you to prove differently, and if you do, they move on.

Modeling scammers seek two things. The first is your child's identity. With this identity they can obtain credit cards, commit crimes, and obtain employment. If they sell the information to another individual, the buyer can obtain loans, purchase cars, or buy homes. The second thing modeling scammers seek is cash and credit card information. If they hook the child and convince the parent, the scammer will require a fee paid up front for their services. Once they have this fee, it is profit, and they move to max out your credit card. Scammers rarely produce any result promised.

If at any point your child drops out or stops communicating with a scammer, think of what he or she is left with. If the child sent a photograph via e-mail, the scammer will take that photograph and circulate it, saying it is another child who was extremely successful working with that modeling agency, and the child in the photograph recommends the agency to all children. If you sent multiple photos, expect to see them sent around the world.

What about in-person modeling agencies? Chances are that they are more often legitimate than fraudulent. A parent can take the agency information and contact the nearest Better Business Bureau (BBB) for their rating and the satisfaction they have provided other customers. This can also be done on the Internet by visiting www.bbb.org. Before you meet with any agency, you can visit the BBB website and check out whether or not they are an accredited agency. My recommendation is to always do your research before visiting or committing to any agency and never allow a child to go to any meeting alone.

Once you give your child's information to someone, your protections will depend on their motives. Even if they are legitimate, how can you be sure they will fully protect your child's personal information? The agencies must be researched before you provide any personal information or funding, and you must have a conversation about the safety of your child's information once provided. If you think this will stand in the way of the furtherance of your child's modeling career, I will tell you that the alternative could be the destruction of your child's financial future. You choose.

QUESTION #94: SHOULD I PAY FOR IDENTITY PROTECTION INSURANCE?

People frequently ask me if they should pay for identity protection. I would first say that from a fraud protection standpoint there are three generic categories of potential identity theft victims:

1. Those who monitor their family's information religiously each and every day looking at bank statements, credit card statements, credit reports, and the details of each monthly bill received.
2. Those who look at some things, check sporadically on other things, and monitor information on a less frequent basis.
3. Those who look at little or nothing at all and believe the odds are that no one would ever want to victimize them.

If you are organized and can remember to follow up every ninety days with one of the credit agencies, as required, to renew your family's fraud alert, then I would say your benefit from signing up for paid identity theft protection will be minimal. One of the largest benefits of an identity theft protection service provider is that they renew the ninety-day fraud alerts for you without action on your part. Some offer other benefits, such as coverage for insurance and attorney fees if there is victimization but the biggest benefit is probably the ninety-day alert renewal.

If you have limited time or desire, and can only sporadically check on your personal and financial information, then I suggest you find the identity theft protection right for you and subscribe today. The costs for services vary, but generally range from approximately $100 to $130 per year, depending on what company you research. If your child has been a victim in the past, you might want to review the different services and choose one to help you monitor your alerts.

If your child has not been a victim, and you have read this book and understand how to obtain your own credit reports and place your own alerts, then you can do most of the same things without a service. The choice is ultimately yours. You can save the money and do it yourself, or pay for the service and have it done for you every ninety days.

Identity theft services offer many services as a whole. If you decide that identity theft protection is right for you, which service is best? There are a multitude of companies, and each company offers different levels of services at different prices. The following are some of the protection services offered by identity theft companies:

- New credit applications
- Family protection
- Insurance
- Checking and savings account alerts
- Address change assistance
- Public record change protection
- Medical identity theft protection
- Negative credit additions
- Lost wallet protection
- Assistance in restoring your identity
- Spyware protection
- Anti-phishing protection

Whether you decide protection is not right for you or you decide that one of the companies you research provides you with exactly what you need, you will want to be free of identity theft. Parents must take to heart the statistical data showing that children are fifty-one times more likely to be victimized than adults. The ultimate question will not be whether child identity thieves will find your children, but rather, when they find them, will they be successful in stealing their identity? Take the steps necessary to keep your family safe from identity theft.

7

FURTHER
RESOURCES

This appendix provides additional resources to help you understand and deal with child identity theft.

QUESTION #95: SUMMARY OF PROTECTIONS FOR UNAUTHORIZED USE OF CREDIT AND DEBIT CARDS

What protections do parents have if they become the victim of credit card or debit card theft? As a general rule, credit cards offer much better protection against unauthorized use when compared to debit cards. To understand why an unauthorized use of a credit card is better than a debit card we must first cover the credit card system and payment for goods. When you go to a department store to buy something and slide your card, the merchant sends a request to the credit card company; once approved, the credit card company pays the merchant.

What is missing from this equation is the fact that you have not yet paid the credit card company for anything. Fraud is usually discovered at this stage by the consumer or the credit card company. Once discovered, the credit card company must either debit the merchant for the fraud, or assume the liability for it and pay the merchant. Most of the time, the credit card company accepts the loss.

The opposite is true, however, for the use of debit cards. When a debit card is fraudulently used, the money is withdrawn directly from the individual's checking account. As soon as the pending charge hits the bank, your balance is reduced by the amount of the payment. The debit card holder is left with reporting the loss to the bank, which leaves the account holder's balance at zero, assuming it was wiped out, until a determination can be made on what the bank is willing to assume as a loss.

If the bank investigates your claim and determines that the theft was reported within two days of the loss, they will charge you for the first fifty dollars and no more. With a credit card, the maximum charge you will pay is fifty dollars, but your period of reporting is greater. Instead of having two days to report your debit card theft, with a credit card you have sixty days. In both cases, if you wait more than two days for a debit card or more than sixty days for a credit card loss, you may have to pay as much as five hundred dollars in unauthorized charges.

Parents want to be able to take care of children's needs. From groceries and doctor bills to shopping at the mall for clothes, parents must have some form of payment when the bill is presented. Payment takes the form of cash, a check, a debit card, or a credit card to pay for their purchases. In most cases, parents have options of what form of payment they carry and prefer. What is critical is that parents carry only what they need and no more.

Carrying extra credit cards, debit cards, or too much cash increases the potential for additional losses should you lose your wallet or purse. It also gives identity theft criminals more to work with should they steal your wallet or purse. Now that we have covered the required charges you must pay for each card lost and used in fraud, you know that carrying more cards than you need will cost you money.

Amounts charged by credit card companies and banks can differ from issuer to issuer. They are also subject to modification from year to year. Review your credit and debit card policies with your bank or issuer. Verify the amounts they might charge should you be victimized. You may be able to shop for a better deal just as you do with your advertised interest rate.

Children follow a parent's example. Setting sound family policies on carrying cards is a step toward teaching them financial responsibility. Adding minimum theft charges to your research on low rates may assist you in selecting a better credit card company or bank. Lastly, remember not to carry your child's personal data unless you need to; this protects it from theft.

QUESTION #96: AS A MILITARY FAMILY, WHAT RESOURCES ARE AVAILABLE TO US?

Armed forces members and their families have military and civilian entities available to help them. Each branch of service sponsors information and support programs for military service members and their families. On-post or on-base options include visiting an Army Community Service Center, Marine Corps Community Services, Fleet and Family Support Center, or Airman and Family Readiness Center. Visits to these services are regardless of your branch affiliation.

Each military installation has a legal office to assist military members with legal affairs. Military lawyers are members of the Judge Advocate General's Corps and commonly referred to as JAGs. JAGs are a resource for both service members and their families, regardless of whether you live on post, on base, or in the local community. If your child is being harassed by a debt collector, and it involves child identity theft, go see your installation JAG.

Your military JAG should be listed in your installation phone directory. You can also find a JAG by searching the websites listed below:

- Air Force—http://www.afjag.af.mil
- Army—http://www.jagcnet.army.mil
- Coast Guard—http://www.uscg.mil/legal
- Marine Corps—http://www.marines.mil/unit/judgeadvocate/Pages/ Home/SJA_to_the_CMC.aspx
- Navy—http://www.jag.navy.mil

What if you are a military family but do not live on a military installation? This is frequently the case with active duty members assigned to recruiting commands. Most universities who have Reserve Officer Training Corps (ROTC) programs or military professional development programs have active duty members assigned. Many active duty military members are also assigned to reserve and National Guard units.

So what do you do if you are not close enough to take advantage of the military installation's services? Active duty service personnel have a sponsor military installation designated to help them regardless of their location. Ask your commander where your support installation is located. National Guard Assistance Centers are also available in every state. To find the National Guard Family Program you can visit www.jointservicesupport.org online.

Your link to military help is never far away. If you are not serving on a military installation, but need legal assistance, use this link to help you find the nearest legal assistance office: http://legalassistance.law.af.mil/content/ locator.php. Military legal JAGs can assist you with all your child identity theft needs. If a letter is required, they can write it. If a phone call stating representation is required, they can handle it. If attorney intervention is required, they can help you.

Still have questions? Turn to Military OneSource at http://www
.militaryonesource.mil. You can also call them at (800) 342-9647. Military
OneSource is available to active duty, reserve, and National Guard members
and their family members. The Military OneSource consultants can make
referrals on a wide range of issues, including identity theft and child identity
theft. They can direct you to resources in person, via telephone, or on the
Internet. Military OneSource is a great resource for military families.

QUESTION #97: SAMPLE LETTERS TO CREDIT AGENCY AND BUSINESS

Date
Your Name
Your Address
Credit Agency's Name (Equifax, Experian, Innovis, TransUnion)
Agency Address

Dear _____,
This letter is in reference to credit file _____ (Name), Account #
_____. I hereby request under the provisions of the 1977 Federal Fair
Credit Reporting Act that you prove to me in writing the accuracy of the reporting
in this credit report. In accordance with the Federal Fair Credit Reporting Act, you
have 30 days to prove the accuracy contained in the report referenced or remove any
and all information from my report.

I have sent this information via certified mail, return receipt requested, and expect a
response within 30 days. If you do not respond within 30 days, I may exercise my
right to meet with my counsel concerning my legal options.

My contact information for you to call me is as follows: _____
_____
_____

Sincerely,
(Your Name)

CHAPTER 7

Date

Your Name
Your Address
Your City, State, Zip Code

Account #
Name of business or credit issuer
Address

Dear Business,
I am the parent of_____, who is a minor under the age
of 18. I have reviewed the account bill you submitted to my child and have found
what I believe to be a fraudulent charge or charges. I wish to dispute the charge on
[date] _____ on the account in the amount of _____. My child
did not make this charge, and thus may have been the victim of child identity theft.

Please remove all charges associated with this disputed incident and close the account. Upon closure, please notify me in writing at the address provided. Enclosed
are copies of the police and Federal Trade Commission Complaint forms filed.

Sincerely,

Parent's Name

Enclosures: (Provide the business a list of what you are enclosing)

QUESTION #98: JOURNAL LOG SAMPLE

Table 7.1 shows a sample of a journal log. Use this format, or one of your
own, to assist you in tracking businesses, agencies, and individuals you
contact in reference to your child's identity theft victimization. A journal
provides you with a record of contacts and assists you in organization.

QUESTION #99: WHERE CAN I FIND OTHER
RESOURCES ON CHILD IDENTITY THEFT?

I embarked on my quest to write this book because, as a law enforcement
investigator, I saw that this crime was occurring but could not find resources

Table 7.1.

Date	Contact	Telephone	Address	Comments

on its aspects and intricacies. I attempted to research the topic very diligently, but found that there were no books in print on the specific subject of child identity theft, and few websites that even mentioned it as a crime.

What I did find was quite a few resources on identity theft committed against adults. Not many of the identity theft books on the market even mention child identity theft. The books that do mention child identity theft reference child identity theft as a subtopic with a broad description. What I found lacking are the elements of the crime and the steps you need to take to protect your child as a parent, guardian, school administrator, service provider, and so on.

Though finding information on child identity theft was difficult, multitudes of articles detail the thousands upon thousands of children victimized each year and their stories are available throughout the world. These articles were found on the Internet on magazine, television station, and newspaper sites. The articles were detailed in their description of children and their victimization, as well as their financial ruin.

A common trend discovered was that identity theft services were capitalizing on the lack of information available and were sponsoring websites and articles on the topic of child identity theft. The information was geared toward making the reader believe that the answer to their fears would be found in purchasing their protection product. In a previous question, the issue of purchasing or not purchasing identity theft services was addressed. In looking for a resource, I look to see if the website tells you all of the truth, such as that the ninety-day credit alert, for which the services charge, can be done for free by the citizen.

These types of issues are of concern and need to be addressed. One of the first things I look for in child identity theft websites, articles, or handouts is who sponsors them. If it is an identity theft protection service, then I am skeptical about the information contained in the publication. Public service entities and businesses that partner with identity theft service providers need to go the extra mile and ensure that all facts are exposed to the reader. If that is done, then the sponsor and the business gain credibility with the public and deserve the respect and business the publicity generates.

Not all sites require sponsors. Nonprofit and government resource sites are available on the Internet to provide information on child identity theft. Examples of nonprofit and government sites are:

- Identity Theft Resource Center—http://www.idtheftcenter.org
- Federal Trade Commission—www.ftc.gov
- Privacy Rights Clearinghouse—http://www.privacyrights.org

Information on child identity theft is limited. As knowledge grows within law enforcement communities, more information will become available to the public. This book can be your one-stop resource for all known aspects of child identity theft. It has been written for parents, guardians, teachers, law enforcement officers, medical professionals, and community leaders.

Child identity theft is an increasingly large portion of the almost ten million cases of identity theft each year. Adults do not suffer the age verification problems and extended years of victimization that children do. Use the information this book offers as your child identity theft reference guide.

NOTES

CHAPTER 1: UNDERSTANDING CHILD IDENTITY THEFT

1. AllClear ID. 2011. "Child Identity Theft Stories: Real Cases from Our Customers." Accessed April 7, 2012. https://www.allclearid.com/blog/child-identity-theft-stories-real-cases-from-our-customers.

2. *Good Morning America*. 2010. "America's Money: Parents Stealing Kids' Identities an Alarming Trend." Accessed April 7, 2012. http://abcnews.go.com/GMA/MellodyHobson/americas-money-parents-stealing-kids-identities-alarming-trend/story?id=11157173#.T4B22dlc-So.

3. Javelin Strategy and Research. 2009. "Latest Javelin Research Shows Identity Fraud Increased 22 Percent, Affecting Nearly Ten Million Americans: But Consumer Costs Fell Sharply by 31 Percent." Accessed April 7, 2012. https://www.javelinstrategy.com/news/777/222/Latest-Javelin-Research-Shows-Identity-Fraud-Increased-22-Percent-Affecting-Nearly-Ten-Million-Americans-But-Consumer-Costs-Fell-Sharply-by-31-Percent/d,pressRoomDetail.

4. *ABC News/Money* 2011. "Proposal to Protect Children's Identities Sparks Debate among Privacy Advocates." Accessed August 7, 2011. http://abcnews.go.com/Business/child-identity-theft-17-10-solution/story?id=14073713.

5. Carnegie Mellon CyLab. 2011. Accessed April 7, 2012. http://www.cylab.cmu.edu/files/pdfs/reports/2011/child-identity-theft.pdf.

6. The Gallup Organization. 2005. "Identity Theft: How Big a Problem?" Accessed April 6, 2012. http://www.gallup.com/poll/18493/Identity-Theft-How-Big-Problem.aspx.

7. KSL TV 5, Salt Lake City, Ut. 2011. "Protecting Kids against ID Theft a Grim Reality." Accessed April 7, 2012. http://www.ksl.com/?nid=148&sid=15096034.

8. Carnegie Mellon CyLab. 2011. Accessed April 7, 2012. http://www.cylab .cmu.edu/files/pdfs/reports/2011/child-identity-theft.pdf.

9. Federal Trade Commission. 2006. "Identity Theft Report." Accessed April 5, 2012. www.ftc.gov/os/2007/11/SynovateFinalReportIDTheft2006.pdf.

10. U.S. Department of Justice 2011. "Stolen Futures: A Snapshot on Child Identity Theft." Accessed August 30, 2012. http://www.ovc.gov/pdftxt/Article _ChildIDTheftSnapshot.pdf.

11. National Commission on Terrorist Attacks upon the United States. 2002. Accessed April 7, 2012. http://www.9-11commission.gov/report/911Report.pdf.

12. WWBT NBC 12. 2012. Accessed April 7, 2012. http://www.nbc12.com/ story/16960306/woman-sentenced-to-14-years-in-fake-id-ring.

13. Federal Trade Commission. 2007. "2006 Identity Theft Survey Report." Accessed April 8, 2012. http://www.ftc.gov/os/2007/11/SynovateFinalReport IDTheft2006.pdf.

14. *Newsweek* magazine. 2009. Accessed April 7, 2012. http://www.thedaily beast.com/newsweek/2009/02/06/sabotaged-by-the-system.html.

15. California Office of Privacy Protection. 2011. "A Better Start: Clearing Up Credit Records for California Foster Children." http://www.privacy.ca.gov/ consumers/foster_youth.pdf.

16. DenverPost.com. 2011. Accessed April 7, 2012. http://www.denverpost .com/nationworld/ci_19077880?IADID=Search-www.denverpost.com-www .denverpost.com.

17. Ronald Mortensen. 2009. "Illegal, but Not Undocumented: Identity Theft, Document Fraud, and Illegal Employment." Accessed February 29, 2012. www .cis.org/IdentityTheft.

18. Ibid.

19. Federal Trade Commission. 2007. "2006 Identity Theft Survey Report." Accessed April 8, 2012. http://www.ftc.gov/os/2007/11/SynovateFinalReport IDTheft2006.pdf.

20. U.S. Federal Trade Commission. 2008. "Federal Criminal Laws." Accessed April 5, 2012. http://www.ftc.gov/bcp/edu/microsites/idtheft/law-enforcement/ federal-laws-criminal.html.

21. U.S. Federal Trade Commission. 2008. "State Criminal Laws." Accessed April 5, 2012. http://www.ftc.gov/bcp/edu/microsites/idtheft/law-enforcement/ federal-laws-criminal.html.

CHAPTER 2: RECOGNIZING HOW CHILD
IDENTITY THEFT HAPPENS

1. U.S. Social Security Administration 2012. "Fact Sheet: Change to the Public Death Master File (DMF)." Accessed September 7, 2012. http://ssa-custhelp.ssa.gov/app/answers/detail/a_id/149/kw/Change%20to%20the%20Public%20Death%20Master%20File%20%28DMF%29.

2. Social Security Bulletin, Vol 64, No.1 2001/2002. "The Social Security Administration's Death Master File: The Completeness of Death Reporting at Older Ages." Accessed August 30, 2012. http://www.ssa.gov/policy/docs/ssb/v64n1/v64n1p45.pdf.

3. *Marketwatch* 2010. "Identity Fraud Nightmare: One Man's Story." Accessed August 30, 2012. http://articles.marketwatch.com/2010-02-10/finance/30765048_1_new-bank-debit-identity.

4. Technolog on NBCNews.com 2011. "Study: Android malware up 400 percent." Accessed September 8, 2012. http://www.nbcnews.com/technology/technolog/study-android-malware-400-percent-123268.

5. Security on NBCNews.com 2011. "Malware infects more than 50 Android apps." Accessed September 8, 2012. http://www.msnbc.msn.com/id/41867328/ns/technology_and_science-security/t/malware-infects-more-android-apps/#.

6. *StarTribune*. 2011. "Stolen Laptop Puts Thousands at Risk of Identity Theft." Accessed April 9, 2012. http://www.startribune.com/lifestyle/health/130644048.html?source=error.

7. The Ponemon Institute. 2009. "The Cost of a Lost Laptop." Accessed April 9, 2012. http://www.ponemon.org/local/upload/fckjail/generalcontent/18/file/Cost%20of%20a%20Lost%20Laptop%20White%20Paper%20Final%203.pdf.

CHAPTER 3: DETECTING AND REPORTING
IDENTITY THEFT

1. Federal Trade Commission 2006. "Identity Theft Report." Accessed April 5, 2012. www.ftc.gov/os/2007/11/SynovateFinalReportIDTheft2006.pdf.

2. U.S. Postal Inspection Service. 2012. Accessed April 5, 2012. www.postalinspectors.uspis.gov.

3. Ibid.

4. *Army Times*, 2012. "Pentagon to Phase Out SSN's on ID Cards." Accessed March 17, 2012. http://www.armytimes.com/news/2008/04/military_id _cards_040408w/.

CHAPTER 4: DEALING WITH CHILD IDENTITY THEFT

1. Associated Press. 2012. "U.S. Says Tax-Related ID Theft Complaints on the Rise." Accessed April 14, 2012. www.http://finance.yahoo.com/news/us-says-tax -related-id-174906354.html.

2. Wikipedia, The Free Encyclopedia. 2012. "Credit Bureau." Accessed 2012. http://en.wikipedia.org/wiki/Credit_bureau.

3. U.S. Code 2003. Accessed August 30, 2012. http://uscode.house.gov/ uscode-cgi/fastweb.exe?getdoc+uscview+t13t16+1988+0++%2815%20USC%20§% 201681c–2%20-%20Block%20of%20information%20resulting%20from%20identity %20theft%29%20%20%20%20%20%20%20%20%20%20.

4. Social Security Administration 2012. Accessed September 11, 2012. www .ssa.gov/history/ssn/firstcard.html.

CHAPTER 5: COPING WITH THE EMOTIONAL FALLOUT FROM CHILD IDENTITY THEFT

1. Javelin Strategy and Research. 2012. "Child Identity Theft Study, October 2008." Accessed March 4, 2012. http://www.debix.com/docs/Child_ID_Theft _Study_2008.10.pdf.

2. U.S. Department of Justice, Office of Justice Programs, 2012. Accessed March 6, 2012. http://www.ojp.usdoj.gov/ovc/pubs/ID_theft/growingtrends.html.

CHAPTER 6: PREVENTING CHILD IDENTITY THEFT

1. *New York Times*, 2007. "A 17-Year Nightmare of Identity Theft Finally Results in Criminal Charges." Accessed August 31, 2012. http://www.nytimes .com/2007/04/13/us/13idtheft.html.

2. American Bar Association, 2007. "Arrest Made in a 17 Years Long ID Theft." Accessed September 14, 2012. http://www.abajournal.com/news/article/ arrest-made-in-a-17-years-long-identity-theft/.

196

RESOURCE LIST

Child identity theft is a new, more lucrative subset of the overall crime of identity theft. Because of this fact, resources devoted exclusively to child identity theft are very limited or nonexistent. I have included a resource list that will give you a starting point to begin your research and point you in the right direction.

RESOURCES

AnnualCreditReport.com
    This is a website providing a centralized service for consumers for obtaining free credit reports. This site was developed by the three major credit reporting agencies: Equifax, Experian, and TransUnion. Website: www.annualcreditreport.com

Carnegie Mellon University Cylab
    This organization does research and education on cybersecurity issues for both the public and private sector. Website: http://www.cylab.cmu.edu

Consumer Military Sentinel
    This is part of the Consumer Sentinel Network and a resource for law enforcement officers who deal with military victims of child identity theft

and identity theft. The Consumer Sentinel provides a secure online data-base of millions of consumer complaints. The Consumer Military Sentinel is operated by the U.S. Federal Trade Commission. Website: www.ftc.gov/sentinel/military/index.shtml

econsumer.gov

econsumer.gov is an initiative of the International Consumer Protection and Enforcement Network (ICPEN). ICPEN is a network of currently twenty-eight governmental organizations involved in the enforcement of fair trade practice laws and other consumer protection activities. econsumer.gov is a portal for victims as consumers to report complaints about online and related transactions with foreign companies. Website: http://www.econsumer.gov/english

Federal Bureau of Investigation (FBI)

This is an investigative federal law enforcement agency that investigates white-collar crime, terrorism, cyber crime, public corruption, major thefts, organized crime, and other serious violations. The FBI is an investigative arm of the U.S. Department of Justice. Website: www.fbi.gov; mail: FBI Headquarters, 935 Pennsylvania Avenue NW, Washington, D.C. 20535; phone: (202) 324-3000

Federal Trade Commission

This government organization is dedicated to preventing business practices that are unfair, anticompetitive, or deceptive to consumers. The website provided is a one-stop shop to learn about the crime of identity theft and report victimization. Website: www.ftc.gov/bcp/edu/microsites/idtheft; phone: (877) FTC-HELP (382-4357)

ID Safety Resources

This is a website sponsored by the International Association of Chiefs of Police. It is an informational resource for both consumers and law enforcement in dealing with identity theft. Website: http://www.theiacp.org/idsafety/enforcement/resources/

Identity Theft Assistance Center (ITAC)

This is a consumer advocate website sponsored by the Financial Services Roundtable. Members of ITAC offer free assistance to victims of suspected identity theft. Website: www.identitytheftassistance.org

Identity Theft Resource Center (ITRC), San Diego, California
This is a nonprofit organization dedicated exclusively to understanding identity theft and related issues. Website: www.idtheftcenter.org; phone: (888) 400-5530; e-mail: itrc@idtheftcenter.org

Internal Revenue Service
This website provides consumers with tax information and reporting of tax-related fraud. Website: www.irs.gov

International Association of Chiefs of Police (IACP)
This is a resource for law enforcement officers worldwide. The IACP provides information on training, leadership, legislation, grant funding, and more. Website: www.theiacp.org

Internet Crime Complaint Center (Ic3)
This site is a partnership between the Federal Bureau of Investigation and the National White Collar Crime Center. The organization serves as a means to receive complaints of cyber crime, intellectual property rights matters, computer hacking, espionage, and extortion. Website: www.ic3.gov

Interpol
This site is an international policing organization where law enforcement agencies and professionals from around the world work to solve crime and make the world safer.
Website: http://www.interpol.int/

National Criminal Justice Reference Service
A federally funded resource offering research on crime topics. Website: www.ncjrs.gov

National Do Not Call Registry
A website for registering telephone numbers at which you desire not to receive further telemarketing phone calls. After you visit the website, register your phone number, and confirm by e-mail, telemarketers are not allowed to call the phone number. Website: https://www.donotcall.gov

Privacy Rights Clearinghouse

This California corporation provides information on consumer advocacy and consumer information dealing with privacy rights and privacy-related complaints. Website: www.privacyrights.org

United States Department of Justice

This agency provides oversight for both investigation and prosecution of federal crimes. The Department of Justice provides resources for information involving crime statistics, case law, and more. Website: www.justice.gov

U.S. Postal Inspection Service

This is a federal law enforcement agency dedicated to protecting the postal system, postal employees, and postal customers. The agency investigates mail fraud, mail theft, identity theft, dangerous mail, and violent crimes. Website: https://postalinspectors.uspis.gov

U.S. Secret Service

The mission of this federal law enforcement agency is to protect America's financial infrastructure. They investigate financial institution fraud, computer and telecommunications fraud, false identification documents, access device fraud, advance fee fraud, electronic funds transfers, money laundering, and more. Website: www.secretservice.gov

Utah Attorney General's Child Identity Protection (CIP) Program

This is a website intended to prevent identity thieves from using the personal information of Utah children to obtain fraudulent credit. Website: https://cip.utah.gov/cip/SessionInit.action

CREDIT REPORT RESOURCES

Equifax—Website: www.equifax.com
Experian—Website: www.experian.com
TransUnion—Website: www.transunion.com

INDEX

ABOUT THE AUTHOR

Robert P. Chappell, Jr., is a twenty-seven-year veteran law enforcement officer. He started his career with the Blacksburg, Virginia, Police Department in 1985. In 1986, he was honored with the Virginia Chiefs of Police Award for Valor in the Line of Duty. Chappell began his career with the Virginia State Police in 1987, where he has worked for the past twenty-five years. He has served in both the Bureau of Criminal Investigations and the Bureau of Field Operations as a trooper, narcotics special agent, sergeant, first sergeant, assistant special agent-in-charge, and currently serves as a lieutenant. Chappell is considered to be an expert in the field of child identity theft.

Chappell is a veteran of the armed forces, having served twenty-five years with the United States Army Reserve. He retired in 2008 as a Lieutenant Colonel. Chappell's military awards include the Bronze Star, Army Combat Action Badge, 101st Airborne Air Assault combat patch, 11th Armored Cavalry combat patch, and the 3rd Armored Cavalry Regiment Order of the Combat Spur. Chappell is married and resides in Roanoke, Virginia, with his family.